THE
PROMISCUOUS
TEENAGER

THE
PROMISCUOUS
TEENAGER

By

DANIEL T. GIANTURCO, M.D.

Associate Professor of Psychiatry
Duke University Medical Center
Durham, North Carolina

and

HARMON L. SMITH, B.D., Ph.D.

Professor of Moral Theology
Duke University Divinity School
Durham, North Carolina

CHARLES C THOMAS • PUBLISHER

Springfield • Illinois • U S A

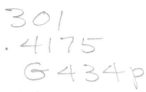

Published and Distributed Throughout the World by

CHARLES C THOMAS • PUBLISHER

Bannerstone House

301-327 East Lawrence Avenue, Springfield, Illinois, U.S.A.

©*1974, by* CHARLES C THOMAS • PUBLISHER

ISBN 0-398-03117-7

Library of Congress Catalog Card Number: 74-6473

*With THOMAS BOOKS careful attention is given to all details of
manufacturing and design. It is the Publisher's desire to present books that are
satisfactory as to their physical qualities and artistic possibilities and
appropriate for their particular use. THOMAS BOOKS will be true to those
laws of quality that assure a good name and good will.*

Printed in the United States of America

RN-10

TO D.S.G. and B.W.S.

FOREWORD

SOME of our friends have ventured to express, quite candidly at times, their consternation (and occasional disbelief!) that the two of us — one a psychiatrist and the other a theologian — should undertake, as coauthors, a venture of this sort; so an *apologia pro libro nostro* probably deserves brief mention here as well.

We have responded to these gentle rebukes for such an outrageous partnership principally in two ways. At an existential dimension both of us have long had a serious and sustained interest in helping people to achieve a sense of direction, purpose, and responsibility in their personal lives. We are also just now, coincidentally, parents of teenage children and therefore caught up in the wide range of activities and concerns which claim their attention at this juncture of their lifetime. But beyond these shared commitments, we manage to arrange an infrequent game of golf together; and it was during one of these, in fact, that the project which has issued in this book was suggested. At another level, we have come to believe that there is perhaps greater need now than ever before for genuine interdisciplinary and interprofessional collaboration, if we are to address in any authentically relevant and responsible way the issues which most deeply concern modern people. The acquisition and accumulation of information is occurring at such accelerated rates that it is no longer reasonable to suppose that any single discipline alone can adequately assimilate and wisely apply all the pertinent data to that range of human affairs which is affected by it. So we need each other; and, acknowledging that, we need to learn how together we can offer services which neither of us alone could provide.

We have therefore explored here the psychological, social, and ethical dimensions of teenage sexuality on the assumption that sexual activity engenders important decision-making for a comprehensive cluster of interested and involved persons — teenagers themselves, their parents, physicians, and all those other people who touch the lives of the young. We think this, then, a constructive enterprise; and we do not regard sexually active teenagers as "bad seed" or "demonic" or any of the other epithets which so thoughtlessly and maliciously label them. Indeed, to the contrary, our experience is that these youngsters are, on the whole, potentially productive, responsible, and useful citizens.

The chapters which follow are straight-forward and self-explanatory. We have not attempted an exhaustive study and discussion of adolescence. To have done so, we would have necessarily included material on dreams in adolescence, more detailed case histories, more extensive recommendations for treatment, fuller discussion of psychological development, and other cognate materials which are somewhat beyond our immediate interest here.

Our intention has been to provide a helpful resource for parents and counselors who perforce work with the young in order, eventually, to help teenagers themselves achieve their own mature and responsible self-understanding and self-direction in the conduct of their sexual life. To that end we have not ventured to prescribe a list of rights and wrongs or do's and don't's. Instead of decreeing sexual behavior, we think it rather more fitting that people think and act in ways that are appropriate to their own self-concept.

ACKNOWLEDGMENTS

MANY persons have contributed to this book during the course of its preparation and we are happy to acknowledge here our debt to some of them. Our colleagues at Duke — particularly Dr. Ewald W. Busse, Chairman of the Department of Psychiatry, and Dr. George W. Maddox, Director of the Center for the Study of Aging and Human Development — have provided support and encouragement for which we are grateful. And we express a special thanks to Dr. Bingham Dai, Emeritus Professor of Psychiatry, for years of helpful teaching and counsel.

Our students have patiently listened to, and enthusiastically criticized, our work. We have profited from that, and believe that what we have written has been refined by their questions and observations.

The cooperation and assistance of the subjects of this book — those promiscuous teenagers whom we studied and about whom we have written — together with their families, has eased our task. These persons have enriched our experience and provided invaluable resource, and we are conscious now, as we were during the months of writing, of our uncommon indebtedness to them.

Jeanetta Radford and Justine Martin, of the Cherry Hospital, were a great help in securing the illustrations we have used. Finally, we express our particular gratitude to Mrs. Hannah Gantt who played a very special role both by giving us the benefit of her experience as wife and mother and converting some very untidy drafts into an orderly typescript.

D.T.G.
H.L.S.

CONTENTS

THE
PROMISCUOUS
TEENAGER

Chapter One

THE NEW SEXUAL FREEDOM

THAT we live in a society which is increasingly characterized by public permissiveness and private parole from traditional standards and sanctions is due, some say, to the Pill and saturation by mass media. These influences, of course, are undeniable. But there is a larger perspective within which our changing sexual mores need to be cast.

Both the Pill and mass media are products of an increasing scientific and technological sophistication which, at virtually every level of theory and practice, makes new knowledge available to us and correspondingly increases our freedom for choices and actions. Before the Pill, fear of pregnancy provided certain restraints toward sexual intercourse that now, after the Pill, are largely groundless. The Pill, of course, is not one hundred percent effective as a contraceptive; but it is effective enough to make the prospect of pregnancy considerably more remote for those who use it than for those who don't.

Similarly, the discovery of antibiotics has gone quite a way toward relieving the fears associated with venereal disease. VD is still a possible consequence of casual sexual liasons; but old fears of infection are diminished in proportion to our capacities for prevention and cure. Moreover, the automobile has revolutionized sexual behavior and attitudes by providing both convenient transportation to a discreet rendezvous and a kind of portable privacy. And so it goes. Scientific and technological discovery and innovation have surely contributed to our emancipation from the old fears of conception, infection, and detection.

THE GENERATION GAP

But perhaps even more important than developments like these is the awareness that liberation from these restraints has been

3

accompanied by corresponding challenges to conventional social and moral teachings. New scientific and technical achievement, which gives us an increasing measure of control over our destiny, also offers alternatives to customary authorities. Therefore, what was once authoritative for many teenagers and their parents — specifically the traditional values of American culture — tend now to be supplanted by another sovereignty; and the prospect of "thinking and deciding for myself" is an attractive alternative to being told what to think and do by someone else!

The challenge of which we speak is not, however, merely the work of scientific and technical advance, and it is naive and simplistic to think so. In many ways, the challenge is more profoundly rooted in the deep moral awareness of many people (and we think especially teenagers) that the "older generation," which includes their parents and society at large, has frequently acted in bad faith and often failed the great moral tests of the twentieth century. Vietnam and Cambodia, racism and sexism, poverty and Watergate are only a few of the social and political crises which have occurred during the lifetime of teenagers and which demonstrate the inability or unwillingness of the "system" — the authority of the generation over thirty — to deal responsibly with the distance between the American creed and America's deeds. The hypocrisies and self-contradictions of the old authorities have played a significant role in creating the generation gap and in engendering, particularly among young people, a profound lack of respect toward both the traditional teachings of the society and its moral authority.

We call this situation *anomie* — literally, without law; but the concept is much broader and deeper than mere lawlessness. *Anomie* is the absence of any corporate authority; it is the death of meaning, the birth of autonomy; the moral equivalent of "every man for himself." And the image which this word evokes is not so much that of men and women who are free now to go where they were once forbidden to go, or do what they once were forbidden to do, as it is of people foundering in a moral fog — undirected and (more or less frantically) searching for purpose and direction. The consequence of this condition is that there is no operative consensus regarding values or actions or sanctions. Instead, there is

Figure 1. A fifteen-year-old male patient's drawing done following discussion of sexual relations.

only a tenuous social consciousness which, at the pragmatic level, sets limits chiefly in terms of what the traffic will bear.

NUDITY

It is in this context that liberation from conventional sexual restraints is both possible and (because of its *un*conventionality) highly visible to the public eye. The topless craze is a case in point. Some cultures have celebrated the beauty of the living human body; ours has not. In fact, until very recently, our society has repressed public display of the naked female breast except in painting and sculpture. Anybody really curious about this feature of female anatomy, however, could have that curiosity satisfied (at least in our major cities) by leering at the statue of Justice on the courthouse facade. Meantime, however, we have simultaneously employed every ingenious device we could imagine and construct to emphasize, and usually exaggerate, women's breasts. Brassieres with padding and "uplift," blouses with deep and revealing decolletage, sweaters stretched to fibre-limits over straining bosoms — we have made it impossible to ignore breasts and at the same time declared that looking is somehow not nice!

Some state courts have defined obscenity in terms of an imaginary line which extends across a woman's chest just above the areolae: any exposure of flesh *below* that line is held in these states to be a lewd display which excites prurient interest, and it is therefore illegal! Given such inventive rationalizations of modesty, it is hardly surprising that emancipation from old restraints regarding nudity should witness, as one of the first alterations in mores, complete exposure of the naked female breast. Beyond this more or less predictable response, however, it is even arguable that such a change is potentially salutary. In contradistinction to those millions of American boys who grew up imagining that every girl had a steel staple imbedded in her navel just like the foldout showed, millions more are now aware that the female breast is not necessarily the tortured and disfigured thing that whalebone, wiremesh, and foam rubber have represented it to be.

Public nudity is quite obviously increasing in our society, and there is probably no reason to suppose that this trend will not continue into the foreseeable future. Total nudity on the stage and a wide assortment of auto-, homo-, and heterosexual situations in films indicate that exposure of the human body is no longer restricted to the underground. Indeed, if there were any doubt of that, the world of fashion has provided what would appear to be the ultimate social sanction with see-through blouses and topless dresses. But nakedness, as any thinking person knows, can be employed in many ways and for many purposes; so it is clearly not nakedness alone that raises questions about honesty, virtue, respectability, and all the rest, but the uses to which nakedness is put. If nudity depersonalizes and exploits, we tend to reject it as a negative value; if, on the other hand, nudity humanizes and enriches, we tend to affirm it. What is then at issue is not nakedness per se, but the meaning which attaches to nakedness.

OBSCENITY

Similarly, the resurgence of grafitti and other behavior which is conventionally labeled "obscene" raises important questions about the ways in which words and actions are perceived. We have already suggested that there is not always a neat correspondence of meaning between certain words and actions, and we will try to show later how recognition of this shift is crucial to diagnosis and treatment of teenagers with sexual problems.

Rape, for example, is a word which is repulsive and ugly because it signifies an action that is dehumanizing, violent, and unloving. Rape is also a word that commonly carries with it distinctive sexual connotations: it conventionally describes forcible sexual intercourse, is attributed almost exclusively to action by males, and is uncritically assumed to occur outside marriage. But the meaning of rape, even in the vocabulary of teenagers, far exceeds this narrow definition — minds can be raped, as lock-step educational processes show; the environment can be raped, as our current ecologic crises show; the human spirit can be raped, as various forms of cultural discrimination show.

Words surely connote actions and behavior, attitudes and affections; but more importantly, the meaning of language lies in its relational aspect. Thus what is obscene and ugly and vulgar is

Figure 2. A drawing by a sixteen-year-old male during art class for emotionally disturbed teenagers.

Figure 3. Grafitti on bedroom wall of disturbed teenager.

whatever denigrates human persons; and what is lewd and unchaste and immodest is whatever violates human dignity and value. It is on such a predicate as this, we think, that many of today's young people consider the carnage of war and the debasement of persons in an elitist society unspeakably more obscene than toilet-wall grafitti or stag movies.

SEXUAL ACTIVITY

Emancipation from old restraints, however, is seldom an

unmixed blessing; and behavioral patterns change, as well as the meaning we attach to language. For example, in a time character- ized by liberation from conventional sexual inhibitions, it might be expected that coital activity among teenagers would increase. Survey data on sexual behavior in a national sample of never- married females, ages fifteen through nineteen, indicate that this is the case and, moreover, that premarital intercourse is beginning at progressively younger ages (1, 2). The same data suggest further that the extent of premarital intercourse is growing, and that about twenty-five percent of the unmarried females in this age group (15-19) have had intercourse. Not surprisingly, there appears also to be a proportionate increase at each age — fourteen percent having had intercourse by age fifteen, forty-six percent by age nineteen.

Perhaps even more striking, in some ways, is the low refusal rate for permission to interview teenagers about their sexual behavior. When we recall the furor raised over Dr. Kinsey's early interviews, the apparent cooperativeness and equanimity of these subjects, together with their parents and others, reveals a great deal about changing attitudes toward sexual behavior.

How to understand and counsel young people in this era of "new sexual freedom" is a vexing question for physicians. In many cases doctors would like to leave this job to others, but the realization that these young patients urgently need consultation about the medical and health dimensions of their sexual activity places a special claim on the physician. If he is to help these patients, the doctor must develop a frank and trusting relationship with them. To be sure, there are many physicians who have not the slightest hesitation about telling young people what they should think and how they ought to behave. Doctors have done their share of encouraging obedience by prescribing sexual conduct without first understanding the young person. Moreover, society itself, awed by the spectacular performance of modern medicine in effecting discoveries and innovations for the allevi- ation of disease, grants almost unquestioning authority to physi- cians in these matters.

This authority has given many scientists the liberty to study sexual behavior under the protective mantle of medicine and thus expand our understanding of an increasingly broad range of sexual phenomena. In addition, psychoanalytic thinking, with its emphasis on mental processes and thoughts which function under low degrees of personal awareness, has made important contributions to understanding how one's previous unique experience influences and colors current sexual behavior. Analytic theories about the ways we actually think and feel, and how these thoughts and feelings shape our sexual behavior, are grounded in numerous detailed observations of individual lives. This work is balanced by social scientists and philosophers who study man as a member of society and a carrier of cultural wisdom. Their insights show us how one's society frequently breeds inhibition, intolerance, and narrowmindedness in sexual matters.

So we are increasingly acknowledging that the work of Dr. Kinsey (3, 4), and his associates, and now more recently that of Dr. Johnson and Dr. Masters (5, 6), is important to those of us who work professionally with the young. Beyond these applications, this information is also important to others of us who simply want to know more about ourselves as sexual beings.

TRUST

It is self-evident that before advising teenagers about their sexual life, the physician must have facts; and this ordinarily necessitates careful, thorough history-taking from patients who are willing to be candid and open about the important details of their lives. For this reason we cannot overemphasize the importance of developing a trusting doctor-patient relationship if the physician is to obtain the information needed to offer competent medical advice.

Trust in adults is not freely dispensed by most teenagers. Embarrassed about the childlike cravings within themselves to depend on others, they tend to be suspicious of "helpful adults" who, they fear, will turn them into children again and take charge of their lives. They also know that such "helpful adults" may, with the best of intentions, inform parents without the teenager's expressed or tacit approval. Indeed, this latter concern is often so great among college students that many school health services have

Figure 4. Wall decoration in room of troubled fourteen-year-old girl who remained absolutely mute for two weeks.

an unwritten policy never to call parents. Instead, the medical staff strongly encourage the teenagers themselves to exercise their own responsibility in these matters.

Younger teenagers, in particular, are often brought (unwillingly) to the doctor by concerned parents. We have seen worried parents coerce or even trick teenagers into a doctor's appointment. In such cases the doctor will frequently be viewed as the parents' agent rather than a helpful friend, which creates an atmosphere hardly conducive to honest, open exploration of the issues. Older teenagers will sometimes be bribed by parents to seek medical aid, as illustrated in the following example.

B., a college sophomore of eighteen, brought her lesbian lover home for a vacation visit. The mother took an instant dislike to this woman who, as the mother discerned, was far too possessive of her daughter. "I didn't like the way she looked at B.," was the way this mother described her feelings; and her worst fears were realized when the daughter carelessly left a love note from this girl on her dresser. (There was probably unconscious intent in this, expressing the daughter's secret wish for her parents to know about and accept her homosexuality.) The angry parents insisted that B. give up her lover; and when she demurred, they threatened to withdraw financial support. Fortunately, before making any final decisions, they sought professional counsel and were advised to let the girl return to college with her lover but with the provision that she enter psychotherapy. The girl reluctantly consented. The opening phase of therapy in this case was characterized by intense distrust, sullenness, and hostility. B. complied with the letter, but not the spirit, of the agreement because she felt coerced into treatment. Happily a successful treatment relationship was eventually established.

Forced treatment (a contradiction in terms?) is not imposed solely by parents. Judges faced with no realistic rehabilitation alternatives frequently offer juvenile offenders the "choice" between a harsh training school or a psychiatric institution. It is not surprising that some offenders will choose the psychiatric institution, not because they understand the need for treatment but merely in order to avoid a more painful loss of liberty.

R., a fourteen-year-old boy, very much admired a young woman whose husband had recently been sent to Vietnam and who lived alone next door. R. broke into her house, stole a pair of panties, masturbated and ejaculated into them, and then left the clearly soiled article on the woman's bed. He was quickly apprehended and brought into juvenile court. The judge who heard the case was confronted with a dilemma: this teenager was like many young sex offenders – shy, somewhat timid, and very inhibited about sexual matters – but the small town was alarmed about "the sex fiend" in its midst. The judge gave R. a choice between training school or voluntary commitment to an adolescent unit. The boy chose the latter; and after admission and evaluation, a course of group therapy was recommended. R., however, resisted these efforts by refusing to speak in therapy. When confronted with his silence, he explained that he was only on the ward to avoid going to training school and wanted no further part of group therapy.

The problem of not trusting doctors or other professionals can, of course, have dangerous implications for teenagers in need of medical care. Many surgeons have had the rather upsetting experience of examining a young female with an "acute abdomen," obtaining a negative reply to their questions about recent sexual contact, and then performing a surgical operation only to discover acute gonococcal salpingitis rather than appendicitis. Gonorrhea is invariably transmitted by sexual contact; and young females who ignore their venereal symptoms, or fail to seek medical consultation and treatment, constitute one important reason for such a high rate of venereally transmitted diseases in the teenage population.

If the physician can ask about sexual experience without communicating embarrassment or condemnation, the teenager will often be more candid. Indeed, in many cases the doctor's matter-of-fact and tactful manner will be an important therapeutic ingredient in relieving the teenager's anxieties. Many teenagers will be more comfortable with physicians of the same sex; and as more women enter medicine and other helping professions, the embarrassment of young girls who have sexual problems should be increasingly alleviated.

AUTHORITY

The image of the doctor in our culture is that of a kindly, helpful, fatherly figure. Such an image presents a particular problem for teenagers, male and female, who are struggling to emancipate themselves from parental authority. This is always a strongly ambivalent struggle between the regressive wishes to be nurtured, loved, and cared for and the powerful drive toward freedom to decide for oneself. Initially such decision-making may be quite selfish. Teenagers may be wrapped up in all their own cravings and desires and look to satisfying their own wishes even at the expense of others. During this stage of life, parents and other adults who are responsible need to set reasonable limits to such autonomy. Hopefully, the loving bond created with parents in the preteen years will be strong enough to temper the rage and defiance such limit setting is heir to.

In any event, in this conflicted setting, the teenager invariably transfers feelings and attitudes to the doctor that are really directed toward the parents. The doctor is therefore frequently viewed as an ominous authority figure who, by a gesture or chance remark, can intimidate and embarrass the teenager. Largely for this reason, many teenagers who do not know the clinical terms to describe sexual organs and function hesitate to use the earthy, expressive street language of sex for fear that they will be chastised. Simultaneously they are not able to reveal their linguistic and conceptual ignorance for fear they will be embarrassed.

Transference of this sort can also serve to inhibit a frank and open conversation about sexual matters. Teenagers are reluctant to confess sexual experience to their parents because they fear punishment, humiliation, and loss of love and support. When these feelings are transferred to the "father figure" physician, they fear a similar rebuke from him. A tactful, sympathetic statement can do much to allay such fears, as this example illustrates:

A teenager of seventeen asked for an appointment; and during the first interview he was a cheerful, smiling person who generally behaved as though he didn't have a care in the world. When asked about this carefree appearance, he readily admitted, "I have a problem but I'm not sure you're a person I can talk to about it." "Is it about sex?" The boy nodded. "Gay sex?" He nodded again. "Well, that's nothing to be ashamed about; it's a common enough situation." With that reassurance, the boy smiled in relief.

Interestingly, this young man had never been able to bring himself to discuss his homosexuality with his parents. After several months of treatment he could discuss the matter with his mother, but he was still too fearful of his father's rejection to talk with him.

Parental authority, which is the source of so much security to the child, frequently becomes a yoke to adolescents and they seek

Figure 5. Portrait drawn by rebellious teenager with many problems.

to cast it off at every opportunity. Their much-sought-for goal is to be autonomous persons, who are securely in charge of their own lives. Not all adolescents rebel, however, and the emotional response to parental authority can continue from childhood into an adolescent placation of parents. There are submissive teenagers whose deepest yearning continues to be pleasing the parents by overly conforming behavior. These adolescents necessarily inhibit their erotic strivings in order to remain childlike in their parents' home; they are very shy in the presence of their peers; and they rarely date. They may immerse themselves in their studies, but not out of genuine intellectual curiosity so much as to escape from developing extrafamilial relationships. Their lack of sexual curiosity and exploration derives less from "goodness" than in intense fear of displeasing their parents.

A common parental configuration associated with such teenagers is a stern, authoritarian father and a meek, submissive mother. In such an atmosphere, and with such role models, these teenagers come to believe that love can be obtained solely by supplication and submission; and they see only one escape: rebellion against the parental values.

Tennessee Williams' poignant story of rebellion, "The Yellow Bird" (7), is a classic description of one such oppressed girl. This daughter of a rigid Protestant minister and his impotent wife finally rebels at the age of twenty-nine, takes up smoking as a protest (the first irretrievable step, in her father's eyes, on the road to perdition), and moves on thereafter to boyfriends, drinking, gambling, and dancing. There was no restraint or prudence once she began, and her life became a monument to the repudiation of all those things her father stood for. She eventually left home and went to New Orleans, where she became a prostitute. She bore a son; who, when he had grown up and traveled the world, returned to his mother with a gift – the yellow bird. She could then die a happy woman because rebellion, while a more healthy response than submission, served only as a prelude to genuine self-discovery.

In this tragic story, the daughter saw the rebellious life as an end in itself. The birth of her son symbolized her eventual growth and maturity into an assertive, autonomous person. And the gift of the yellow bird became the symbol of freedom from the bondage of her past. Finally she was free to be herself.

Rebellion is ordinarily a temporary phase in normal adolescent development, necessary only as the teenager passes from reliance on outer authority (the parents) to inner authority (a self-imposed value system). Eventually young adults can accept parents as simply persons like themselves. They can be realistic about their parents' assets and limitations and go their own way, leaving behind the intimate family life which was so necessary in their formative years.

INTIMACY

The development of trust, and the resolution of authority-autonomy issues, prepares the teenager for the next step in emotional development, which is intimacy. Ordinarily one might expect at this point a discussion of that subject, but we will defer that because intimacy appears to be primarily an adult phenomenon. To be truly lonely and hungry for a mature emotional closeness to another human being has only rudimentary beginnings in the latter part of adolescence. Teenagers project characteristics onto their partners which are partly a product of their own immature emotional needs. Initially young people are satisfied with such romantic and idealistic notions of others. Maturity, however, brings forth more realistic notions of other people, together with a curious paradox: the capacity to be alone, and the genuine hunger for someone with whom one is free to be open and honest.

Hopefully, this report will provide a secure foundation for physicians interested in helping young people with their sexual difficulties. Medical intervention, understanding, judgment, and guidance will frequently be the critical factors in successful resolution of their problems.

Chapter Two

SEXUAL DEVELOPMENT

SEXUAL IDENTITY

THE sexual behavior of human beings is a very complex, and sometimes baffling phenomenon. In part it appears to inhere in physical appearance and genetic structures which are endowed at conception; in part it seems grounded in learning processes which occur during one's lifetime. Some scientists postulate that the earliest years (to ages 2 or 3) are critical in the formation of sexual identity, both in oneself and toward others, because it is during this time that a child learns his or her sexual identity and role (from parents and other intimate associates). Other scientists argue that our psychosexual identity is organized by an inherent somatic sexuality which, while not always manifesting itself clearly at birth, nevertheless provides each of us with a built-in sexual bias (8, 9).

Even if there is no consensus on this question yet, it makes sense to think that the truth is probably "both/and" rather than "either/or". Each of us is endowed, more or less fully, with biochemical and organic structures and systems which objectively define sex. But anatomy and physiology alone are insufficient criteria for defining sexual identity or determining sexual conduct in our culture. We prefer to think that genitals and breasts and the rest of our sexual apparatus are part of what it means to be a person, and that we therefore cannot separate these biological aspects of ourselves from the meaning which we attach to human and personal existence.

On the other hand, each of us acquires at least part (and perhaps even a large part) of his or her sexual identity and understanding from parents. But no more than we are willing to accept the notion that biochemical or organic structures define our sexuality are we willing to grant that our sexuality is merely the product of social or environmental conditioning. So we reject both thorough-going behaviorism and mechanistic naturalism as definitive of our sexual identity; while still acknowledging that both of these aspects of our sexual identity and understanding are important, even indispensable, ingredients in our total sexual awareness.

Long before children become self-conscious about external genitalia, parents have begun to treat them in discrete ways that are calculated to shape their sexual identity. Boys have been given soldier-dolls; girls play with baby-dolls. Boys wear trousers and ties; girls are dressed in frilly blouses and skirts. Among children themselves, studies have shown that sexual differentiation is recognized by two-year-olds, and that children can identify themselves as boys or girls by age three.

It is also the case that as early as age three both male and female children engage in self-stimulation by holding and fondling their sexual organs. Because these children initially feel no guilt, they will (as parents frequently say) "play with themselves" openly in the presence of both adults and children. That they are said to "play with themselves" is itself perhaps a cue to the meaning which parents and other adults attach to this behavior. Somehow "to play" with sexual organs is widely thought to be inappropriate. But children holding and fondling their sexual organs can also stir up old masturbatory conflicts in parents, who typically respond by being either too harsh in their attempts to suppress this behavior or too permissive in their attempts to ignore it totally. Moreover, that children are said to be playing with "themselves" betrays a tendency to locate, however uncritically, selfhood in genitalia; and repressive and suppressive parental responses effectively communicate the erroneous notion that, of all those components which constitute "self," the genitals are most sacrosanct and inviolable. It would be a truer and healthier expression of the way it really is with us if sexual organs, as sexuality itself, were understood to be important − even precon- ditional and indispensable − but not definitive of self.

If we are to have a more adequate understanding of what it means to be a sexual being, to be a man or woman, several factors must be integrated together. Some of these are scientific, some are humanistic — they belong together. The day is long past when scientists can pursue their investigations on the naive and mistaken supposition that "bare facts" and "raw data" function without reference to any system of value or principle of interpretation; and, similarly, the time is gone when humanists can pontificate about human sexuality without acknowledging the best scientific information and having at least rudimentary acquaintance with it.

Initially, then, we need to get straight on what we are talking about, because male-female, masculine-feminine, and man-woman are not synonymous pairs of words. There are feminine females and masculinized females, just as there are masculine males and effeminate males. It is now recognized that there are at least six factors which contribute to a person's sexual identity: (1)chromosomes, (2)gonads, (3)hormones, (4)internal accessory reproductive structures, (5)external genitalia, and (6)assigned sex and rearing. The problem of "appearance" vs. "reality" is a very old one philosophically; and now we are faced with it in terms of sexual identity and development.

These relative biochemical and organic structures, for example, have cultural parallels. Our tendency has been to assume that the sexual behavior patterns which prevail in our culture are natural and therefore right. But anthropological and animal research into sexual conduct reveals that both male and female are capable of a wide variety of behavioral patterns and that the prevalence of one or another practice is very often culture conditioned. Moreover, in the light of advanced medical and psychological information, some sexual behavior that has conventionally (and mistakenly) been credited to a perverse volition is now seen (more accurately) to be related to serious biochemical or organic anomalies and subsequent psychic disabilities over which a person may exercise little or no control. Certain chromosomal studies definitely suggest this hypothesis. And when we further acknowledge that a person's psychosexual orientation is developed and established over the course of many experiences, it is a compelling argument that all of us — and perhaps parents especially — should be acquainted with and sensible of those factors which influence and mold sexual self-understanding.

ADVISING PARENTS

In order to deal with a child's curiosity about genital differences, masturbation, birth, adult sexual relations, and many related matters, parents will need to be advised of the several scientific factors and assisted in linking them with personal understandings of sexuality. Some experts pander to parental anxiety by giving specific prescriptions of what to say and do. Implicit in their ritualized advice is the threat that if you don't say the right thing the child's sexual development will be maimed for life. But a child's sexual development is ordinarily guided more by observation of parental affection and respect toward each other, and toward the child, than anything the parents say specifically. Parents will need, of course, to do some explaining to inquisitive children. Our impression over the years has been that reproduction is the primary, and often the only, feature of sex that gets a thorough airing in home discussions. But, as even children suspect, there is a great deal more to sex than procreation.

Preschool children with adequate social contacts are usually already aware of sex differences. Mutual showing of genitals is common in children. (All children are exhibitionists and modesty is only gradually acquired. It is commonplace that children love to be photographed and to occupy the center of attention.) The presence of the penis in the male and its absence in girls is usually noted proudly, but also often tinged with anxiety by boys and scornfully, but enviously, by girls. Children's curiosities, mutual explorings, and questions about genitals are healthy and normal; and these can provide parents the opportunity to teach the complementary nature of the male-female sexual apparatus, while simultaneously engendering pride in one's own sex and respect for the opposite sex. Parental nudity in front of children, while advocated by some authorities to teach respect for and pride in the body, may often be threatening and seductive to shy children and should be used cautiously.

Holding and fondling of the sexual organs (masturbation) is universal in male and female children and can be seen as early as age three. Since children initially feel no guilt, they will do this openly in front of parents and other children. Children should gently be taught to masturbate in private because such complete self-absorption as masturbation implies leaves no room for others. Masturbation becomes less important as the world around the child becomes more interesting and pleasureable.

Children's questions about the origin of babies may reflect curiosity that needs a simple, truthful response appropriate to the child's age. On the other hand, where the birth of siblings is concerned, children's questions about babies may also be a way of seeking support and reassurance about their parents' love at a difficult time for them. Repetitious questioning may reflect such concerns as "Why do you need a new baby, am I not enough?" and "What are you going to do with me when the new baby comes?" Questions about the origin of babies ordinarily occur later (ages six to eight). The emerging cognitive awareness by children of the world around them leads into primitive reflection on the meaning of their existence. This is the first existential question children pose to themselves and to their parents.

In the preteen years (ten to twelve), children's sexual curiosity turns from birth and procreation to the mechanics of sexual relations. Fantasies of oral impregnation follow, of course, from confusion of stomach and uterus. As adolescence approaches, girls and boys need instruction on menstruation, emission, ovulation, breast and pubic hair growth, voice changes, and sexual urges.

INITIAL SEXUAL EXPERIMENTATION

The emergence of adolescence is signaled by these developments together with an awakening of erotic strivings. An interest and curiosity in others as sexual human beings is then generated, which may initially be satisfied by fantasied relationships where the adolescent's needs for security, admiration, protection, and companionship are evident. Often this interest is centered on persons of the same sex. Early sexual experimentation such as mutual masturbation, breast stimulation, and crural intercourse are frequent with persons of the same sex. That these experiments are homosexual, or that feelings of admiration may be directed toward such people, are not to be confused or equated with adult homosexuality. These experiments and feelings (though often intense) should be properly understood as "practice sessions" with another who is a safe and familiar person.

Even in these first furtive attempts, adolescents often express yearnings and speculations about "the real thing." Nevertheless, masturbation is the principal outlet for the discharge of their sexual tension. Concurrently, and despite widespread efforts by many persons and organizations to dispell the erroneous notions about the dangers of masturbation, adolescents express great embarrassment about their masturbatory activities. "Playing with yourself" is still not entirely acceptable to them because of their conflicting hunger for real relationships. Thus, self-stimulation and fantasies are merely an outlet for the discharge of tension; and as such they are substitute gratifications which adolescents permit themselves only because meaningful sexual relationships are not yet available to them.

Sexual awakening is feared by many parents who see their role as strict prevention of any sexual activity until adulthood. A more responsible approach by parents would be to impart healthy views of sex associated with reasonable limit setting. Therefore, sexual experiences will preferably await the emotional maturity of a secure self-concept (usually in late adolescence) which is needed to maintain a sense of sureness and confidence and inner harmony that allows regrouping of the self after the abandonment of sexual relations.

While some experts advise against specific prohibition of premarital intercourse, it is perhaps too much as Levin (10) states, "to expect young girls and boys to have the wisdom to make decisions in areas where even their elders flounder." The principle of premarital virginity is not dead, but it is best grounded in the recognition that maturity has not yet arrived.

THE CHANGING SELF-PICTURE

Society, particularly among the middle class, places great importance on social concourse with the opposite sex. For example, mothers make sure that even the most awkward youngsters learn to dance; they coach them on what to say and how to behave in social situations; they teach them, in a word, manners. In addition, the sexually segregated school is fast becoming a thing of the past; and dormitories at some of our most prominent colleges and universities have abandoned sexual segregation. As a consequence, teenagers of both sexes are early exposed to each other's thinking, values, and attitudes.

There is also a healthy admixture of cultural values. Girls are more apt to take on traditional masculine interests and ambitions, and boys are learning much earlier than they ordinarily would to appreciate women as people. Traditional views of strongly segregated sexual roles are fast crumbling, particularly among our

Figure 6. Wall decoration in room of teenage girl.

educated young.

Scientific evidence suggests that differences in the self-picture among young men and women are also vanishing. Utilizing such psychological instruments as the Rorschach inkblot test, Dr. Fred Brown (11), a well known psychologist at Mount Sinai Hospital in New York, discovered that during the last decade there has been a radical change in responses to the test. In sum, his studies suggest that men and women are viewing themselves in a more similar fashion. Most male patients in the 1950's saw a particular inkblot as masculine. Now, in contrast, most of his subjects – regardless of sex – identify the same inkblot as feminine. The self-picture of adolescents is changing.

DEPENDENCY AND SHAME

The search for an enduring, stable, relatively favorable self-concept is the central personality problem for the adolescent (12), probably not completely resolved until early adulthood. As adolescence progresses and erotic strivings seek some outlet, incest taboos require that the adolescent live more and more in a society of peers. There teenagers have responsibility and authority to act. Correspondingly, the family assumes less importance as a source of support although it remains a haven of retreat in times of stress. The adolescent is a person in transition from the dependent child state to mature independent adulthood and as a consequence, may experience intense shame when confronted with the reality of dependent needs. The following case illustrates.

A fourteen-year-old teenager was charming and poised with her friends, with whom she discussed clothes and boys and complained about homework and teachers. She played the piano and was studying the clarinet in the school band. She was a considerable help around the home. Her parents considered her mature and responsible. At bedtime she still insisted that her mother tuck her in. She would come to her mother with hands behind her back and eyes lowered (gestures of submission) and ask to be put to bed. Her bed was filled with toy animals, the favorite position occupied by a stuffed panda. On one occasion, her father walked by her bedroom and remarked, "Aren't you too old to be tucked in?"; whereupon the young girl immediately hid her face under the covers in shame.

Adolescents move toward an independent state where they are free to make their own decisions about how they will behave with people. Yet, underlying dependency needs make them reluctant to assume full responsibility for their actions, as this case shows: A fourteen-year-old boy wanted very much to go to the movies on a week night. His parents, concerned about his poor school performance, refused his request and insisted that he do his homework instead. Thereupon the boy threatened to kill himself, went into the bathroom and ingested ten aspirin. His alarmed parents brought him to the hospital, where he was admitted for suicidal observation. The next day he was demanding release, claiming that he "didn't really mean it," and expressing great hostility toward his parents for bringing him to the hospital. The doctor pointed out to him that his behavior appeared to be an attempt to destroy himself and asked what else he had expected concerned parents to do but bring him for help.

PARENTAL CONFLICT

The parents of teenagers are in an equally difficult situation. Should they let the teenager make unwise choices? Should they exercise less restraint? They recognize that their influence is waning at precisely the time when young persons' actions can seriously damage themselves or others. These are not neat and unmixed problems, and each parent must eventually decide on limits that are realistic and enforceable. For example, a college freshman was sharing his apartment with a girlfriend. During the spring break he announced to his family that he was bringing the girl home and that he and she planned to share his old room. His mother replied, "You cannot sleep with that girl under my roof." Since the parents presumably have control over what goes on in their own household, letting the couple sleep together implied sanction and approval. So the parents heartily disapproved; but, on the other hand, they made no serious effort to break up the arrangement at their son's apartment. They reasoned that surely at age eighteen, he could decide for himself about his own conduct.

In any event, they acknowledged that they could not realistically exert control over his actions at such a distance except by refusing him money; and they did not wish to do this. Instead the parents settled on a course of action that preserved their own respect and autonomy, as well as their son's.

The end of adolescence is signaled biologically by ossification of the epiphyseal plate of the tibia. For better or worse, our society knows no such precise demarcation between adolescence and young adulthood. Indeed, quite to the contrary, modern techno-logical society, with its extensive educational requirements, ordinarily prolongs adolescence into the middle twenties!

THE ADOLESCENT AND SOCIETY

Adolescents are, of course, not only individuals but also members of society and carriers of culture. At the core of their being is a primary self-concept (13), a conscious system of attitudes and values which is acquired in the first or family group environment. Thus to discern one's self-concept includes a realistic understanding of impulses, social conscience, and self-protective mechanisms. We must acknowledge that the techniques for comprehending and changing this self-concept are imperfectly understood. Moreover, even to embark on such a venture requires a self-scrutiny so intense that one must have a reservoir of personal strength even to tolerate the procedure.

Efforts to maintain a favorable self-picture, and to integrate the self concept with the environment, lead to behavioral patterns that can isolate the adolescent. Sexual conflict, coupled with an unfavorable self-concept, can lead to anxiety, neurotic symptoms, and often maladaptive behavior. These phenomena inevitably promote further alienation from meaningful relationships with others. It is a generalization, but nevertheless true, that the vocation of adolescence is to develop mature attitudes toward other people so that the adolescent can acquire that sense of self-respect and self-trust which is so essential to a favorable self-concept.

The following example illustrates the applicability of these formulations to a clinical problem:

A sixteen-year-old girl was admitted to an adolescent unit following several days of very strange behavior. She insisted, much to her parents' mystification, that she see a physician but refused to explain her purpose. Once at the physician's office, she would not answer his questions or allow him to conduct an examination. She did demand a pregnancy test because, she said, people were talking about her at school and accusing her of being pregnant. Thereafter, she would no longer leave her home for fear that people were gossiping about her. She became depressed, morose, complained of nausea, and refused to eat. This latter symptom galvanized the parents into action; but before emergency admission could be arranged, she had already refused all food for forty-eight hours.

On the ward she was described as passive, isolated, and withdrawn. She began to consume small portions of food after the staff tube fed her on one occasion. She was uncooperative during the initial psychiatric interview, often staring blankly into space and totally ignoring the examiner's questions. She did complain that there were insects crawling under her skin (a rare symptom sometimes seen in drug addicts, but she was not one). She was the youngest of five children in an intact and very religious family. She was always considered a submissive, dutiful child who tried hard to meet parental expectations by performing well in school, attending church and Sunday School. Indeed, she was an able student and hoped to go to college.

She started dating a college age boy about one year prior to admission. She literally worshipped this boy and chafed increasingly under her parents' strict dating guidelines. In addition, this boyfriend put strong pressure on her to prove her love for him by having sexual intercourse. Although this relationship was in strong conflict with her moral teachings, we learned from her sister that she had recently given in to her boyfriend's demands. Initial diagnosis was schizophrenic reaction, acute undifferentiated type.

Her treatment began with phenothiazine medication and a careful nursing plan to draw her out of her own self-imposed shell. As she slowly recovered under this regimen, treatment evolved around helping her resolve submissive and conforming attitudes toward both her parents and boyfriend. She had been confronted with the conflict of two disparate value systems which she was unable to resolve and which literally "drove her crazy." Accordingly, we set out to help her learn to deal with people and their demands. Our firm clinical opinion was that she had to integrate a value system that was harmonious to her own needs and wishes before she could become a whole person again. Improvement in this case was rapid and dramatic. She left the hospital after six weeks, a much more confident person.

This patient's case is not unique in our experience, and only illustrates the subtle and intricate ties between self-concept development and sexual behavior. That these elements are profoundly interrelated in the self and in relationships with others seems to us self-evident, but too often neglected or forgotten. Emotional maturity and secure personal identity are requisite to healthy personal and interpersonal relationships.

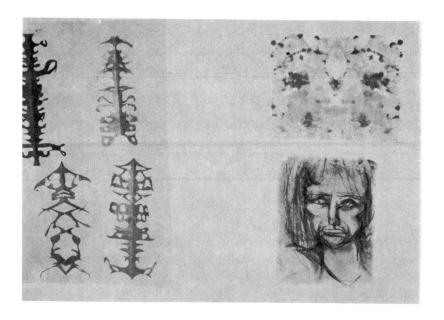

Figure 7. Self-portrait and other drawings of severely depressed teenager.

Chapter Three

MARRIAGE

$\mathbf{W}$HEN parents bring their adolescent children's sexual problems to the physician, an honest and open exploration of the entire family structure is indicated. Not infrequently the physician will uncover a sexual problem between the parents which, if adequately treated and resolved, will allow the parents to approach their adolescent's sexual problem in a more mature and understanding way.

As we pointed out in the previous chapter, the sexual development of children is heavily influenced by their observations of parental affection and respect shown toward each other. Parents must first develop in themselves important values such as intimacy, cooperation, and commitment, and a marital relationship characterized by mutuality. They will then be free to facilitate their teenager's sexual development without being excessively critical or extremely permissive. For these reasons, and because we characteristically reflect upon the meaning and purpose of human sexuality in terms of the conjugal relationship, a brief discussion of sex and marriage is appropriate.

MARRIAGE MANUALS AND SEXUAL DIFFICULTIES

Interest in venereal pleasure and satisfaction is adequately attested to by an abundance of marriage manuals and marriage counselors (some of whom are clearly frauds). These authors and practitioners may be amateur or professional, but they are united by a single overriding purpose: to bring sexual excitement and compatibility to every marriage. There has been great interest recently, for example, in why many wives fail to experience orgasm during intercourse; and that interest has engendered a number of books which prosecute the "inalienable right of every woman to achieve orgasm" and provide clinical hints for its accomplishment. Some authors adopt a more or less mechanical approach and describe in some detail those internal muscles which, if a woman will just conscientiously exercise them for two to twelve weeks, will save her marriage. Others rely on the psychology of sexual surrender and argue that women miss most of the fun in sex simply because they do not "let themselves go."

We noted earlier that we need to be aware of the best technical information available to us. Now we can add that in the measure to which these manuals provide that information they can be gratefully received. Much of this literature does, in fact, show great understanding and sensitivity in discussing the most intimate problems which some husbands and wives face. The difficulty with books of this sort, however, is that they tend to encourage an egocentric and hedonistic approach to life; that is, the whole marital relationship tends to be reduced to its venereal dimension where the crucial question is whether one receives pleasure and satisfaction. Beyond this tendency, there is the corollary suggestion that if pleasure and satisfaction are achieved at a venereal level, everything else will take care of itself.

More likely, the reverse is closer to the truth. A man and a woman who have mutual feelings of tenderness, kindness and concern, who try to help each other, communicate their fears and worries to each other and try to know each other, will eventually develop a mutually satisfactory sexual relationship.

Certainly a sex technique manual, read together and discussed, can serve as an important communication vehicle for learning about each other; but even this enterprise is better guided by mutuality than a wooden following of the author's prescription for sexual nirvana. Sexual difficulties in marriages are ordinarily misunderstandings between a husband and wife. They are a warning that something is amiss – symptoms of a disturbed man-woman relationship.

There are many in our society, particularly males, who would like forthrightly to reject the notion that a wife's lack of responsiveness or orgasm might be a personal problem involving the husband. These men are eager to deny that a misunderstanding or difficulties in communication have occurred. "Go to the doctor and get fixed up," they say to their wives. Interestingly, women do tend to be more open and candid about such things, more ready to admit to difficulties and lack of understanding in their intimate relationships. Men, falsely imbued with the doctrine of performance, see the solution as a "rousing roll in the hay." They interpret their own failure as weakness on their wives' part and only secretly entertain doubts about their own love-making abilities. They think that if only they were Don Jaun or Casanova all would be fine.

In view of such attitudes, it is not difficult to see why such people eagerly seek a magical solution, like a technique or method, to wipe away quickly the unresponsivity which they interpret as a blot on their own self-image. In our society, women (who have been exposed to similar cultural teaching as their men) often see their difficulties in responding in much the same way, that is, as a failure rather than a warning. So they, too, are avid buyers of books that preach a cheap success and are eager visitors to counselors or doctors who offer an instant cure. The truth of the matter is that the resolution of these problems depends less on technique and method than upon patient and disciplined cooperation of partners.

Sexual difficulties looked at in the proper light need not be blights on the characters of the conjugal participants. They provide an opportunity for enriching and deepening the marital relationship with a mutually cooperative and collaborative exploring effort to know each other more fully. The "frigid" woman and the "impotent" man are saying to their respective spouses, "You turn me off! When I'm with you I feel confused, fearful, and guilty!" Honest and open exploration of these issues is a sign of strength and commitment in the relationship, an underlying sureness and confidence that a mutually satisfactory solution can be worked out.

MUTUALITY

Venereal pleasure constitutes an important dimension of marriage – we need not have any doubt about that – but it does not constitute the sum nor exhaust the range of relationships between husband and wife. Mutuality is a sharing, collaborative relationship between a man and a woman. Each is a separate and distinct person in the relationship, yet equal, valued and one. There is no passivity in this relationship, for passivity is merely a subtle form of coercion wherein, by lack of activity, one tries to lever the spouse into meeting immature dependency needs. There is nothing passive, submissive or docile in the mutual relationship. Each is assertive in expressing his or her mature wants and needs, and in meeting the needs of the spouse.

This brings us to another aspect of mutuality — and that is the capacity to tolerate some frustration of individual needs and wishes in order to achieve wholeness. It is demand of the immediate or instantaneous, the "can't wait" or "now," which has no place in the private, personal, mutual relationship but takes sexual expression in the much sought-after, much talked-about, mutuality of orgasm. The mutual relationship bears the gift of sureness and security about the self-role and the role of the spouse.

Frequently couples will describe their struggling years as the "happiest time of our lives." That this is so probably lies in the struggle for existence which drove them into close cooperation. Perhaps the husband was a student. The wife worked to put him through school. Each month, with careful planning, their money had to last — so much for rent, food, books, clothes. Alas, three dollars left over . . . how to spend it . . . a long discussion would ensue and finally a movie would be decided upon and they trooped off happy as clams. Later the same man, now successful, has to have his secretary remind him of his wife's birthday. Or the wife leaves a note to her husband, "I'm playing bridge with the girls — TV dinner is in the oven." The sharing, caring, mutual relationship is lost.

The singleness of man and woman in marriage, moreover, is not arithmetical but organic. They do not swallow up each other in a way that obliterates personal identity. One famous personality described this relationship thusly: "I feel we have an idyllic marriage. We are close without intruding on each other, and that, I believe, is the secret of our happiness."

What does it mean, then, "to love somebody"? To love another person means that the health, well-being, and happiness of that person is now regarded as more important than one's own health, well-being, and happiness. A loving person transcends superficial differences and petty selfishness by giving himself or herself to the other.

COUNSELING COUPLES

Hopefully physicians will not bring unrealistically optimistic ideas of their abilities to alleviate marital problems. For the most part, a sexually conflicted couple is not the "acted upon" recipient of the doctor's skills, as are surgical or medical patients. Physicians best accept the fact that they are unable to "cure" the couple only by the power of their own skills or intellect. Today there is increasing interest among marital counselors in game analysis and theory, where the goal seems to be to outwit the couple's problem and force them into health. Some physicians grasp games theory as meaning that one can lever or manipulate people into "cure" by clever maneuvers, affording, as it were, a certain amount of omnipotence for the doctor.

Counseling for couples requires an adequate grasp of the psychology of men and women, understanding of the concept of mutuality, and the nature of love. Unlike directive advice-giving or a games method therapy, truly helpful physicians do not act upon the couple to impose their own views or methods. Rather their goal is to assist the couple in uncovering the true state of their marital relationship. Once they realize how they are relating, their own intuitiveness will usually grasp the solution. The therapist's task is first to free the minds of the individuals so they can see the truth about themselves and their relationship.

ALTERNATIVE LIVING STYLES

None of us seriously doubts that our time is very different in important ways from any that has preceded us on this earth. We live in an era which is uniquely our own. And while this is not the place to detail all the remarkable ways in which this is such an obvious fact of our lives, it is important for us to acknowledge that ours is a time especially marked by novelty and change. Most important, for our purposes here, are those alterations that are taking place in our understanding of human sexuality and the new practices which are attendant to it.

Today there is no doubt that the conspiracy-of-silence curtain, which so long stifled discussion about sexual activity, has been parted. The initial changes were rung by zoology professor Alfred C. Kinsey (3, 4), whose books on sexual behavior in the late 1940's had a powerful impact. His works stimulated much honest and open exploration of sexual matters, as well as an avalanche of articles and books. Meantime, in our schools and churches, sex education is beginning to be offered to our youngsters, helping them to learn about their bodies and feelings in an atmosphere free of shame and fear.

It is probably laboring the obvious to argue that sexual practices are very different, in certain important ways, from what they were, say, in Queen Victoria's time. For that matter, they are very different from what they were in any earlier time. Old convictions are being challenged; some practices and restraints are being discarded. This is not yet to say whether our sexual practices are better or worse than those of previous generations; it is only to argue that the issues are *ours* and not theirs, and that therefore the ways in which we deal with them must be uniquely referable to our own special circumstances rather than those of another time.

COMMUNAL LIVING

Today, particularly among young people, there is a reawakening of interest in communes. Many experiments in communal living are apparently well-established and thriving. One such commune, organized around the concept of "providing legal aid for the poor," is filled with young lawyers who live together, share housekeeping duties, and pool their money and talents, all to advance their common cause. Many women's liberation advocates see communal arrangements for several couples as a desirable way to share boring and repetitious tasks such as housekeeping, cooking, and child rearing. (Our wives, looking over our shoulders during the writing of this chapter, were not sure they wanted their own children to be cared for by someone who saw child rearing as only tedium and annoyance.)

Still others see the commune experience as a way to resolve the problem of loneliness, or even love. "Just think," one coed told us, "in this commune there are forty people who are interested in me and love me." On the other side, older people usually shudder at the complexities of sharing a personal life with forty people when it is so demanding to share it with just one other person.

A wide variety of sexual styles may be practiced in communal living (14). A frequent pattern is serial monogamy among couples who generally remain faithful to each other by mutual consent for the duration of the relationship, although each partner may occasionally have sexual intercourse with another person. Singles in these communes sometimes enjoy complete sexual freedom. Other communes may practice open sexuality with no limitations on form or structure. There may be couples, threesomes, foursomes, or other combinations.

It need not come as a surprise that the usual dyadic love relationship which our culture sanctions and encourages has come under attack. Many intellectuals, writing in sophisticated journals, are very tolerant, and even advocate alternative living styles. People need to be free, they argue; and therefore they need to be free to love (usually meaning coitus) any time there is mutual interest and consent.

One such young man, espousing this idea, was recently seen by a physician colleague who told us this story: "The young man, a college student, shared an off-campus house with seven free spirits including his coed girlfriend. They agreed that both be free to develop other sexual relationships and this he enthusiastically did with the vigor endowed by his youth. He requested examination because he was sure he had a physical problem . . . a curious abdominal distress likened to a hollow, achy, empty feeling in the 'pit of my stomach.' He was sure he had an ulcer. The story of the development of this curious symptom goes like this: 'I went back to the house a little early after a date with Sally (a new acquaintance) . . . I went up to my room but it was already occupied . . . I switched on the light and found Joan (the girlfriend) and Tom (allegedly his best friend) . . . They were making love and Joan seemed to be really enjoying it.' That evening the young man not only noticed for the first time 'my ulcer' but was impotent with Joan. 'I couldn't make it with her.' Emotionally the young man could not grant his girlfriend the same freedom he so eagerly sought for himself. This open confrontation in the bedroom forced him to face the reality of their relationship, its importance to him, and its inherent contradictions."

SYNERGAMY AND OPEN MARRIAGE

Lovemaking is usually thought to be a very private action between two people in the solitude of a bedroom. There, free from the prying eyes of society, they can be themselves with each other in any way they find mutually satisfactory. Yet, in a time when persons are increasingly called upon to renounce some of their own individuality and privacy for the greater social good, it is not surprising that people have talked and written openly about sexual practices, marital relationships, and living arrangements that involve more than the usual dyadic relationship.

Among these, perhaps the best known is R. R. Rimmer (15), whose novels have explored alternative arrangements to the conventional family structure including bigamy, group marriage, and open-end marriages. This latter form — open-end marriage — includes a marriage plus a structured, sanctioned, adulterous relationship. He calls this "synergamy," which suggests that the adulterous relationship incorporates a genuine emotional commitment. Rimmer argues, moreover, that group marriages create an adventurous, vital life for the participants, who stand to profit from greater self-knowledge even if the relationships do not endure. And he insists that this is not adultery since the people involved give each other permission for other sexual relationships.

Another alternative to conventional monogamous marriage is "open marriage," as proposed by the O'Neills (16). They studied the marriage ideas of four hundred primarily middle-class people, aged seventeen through seventy-five, and concluded that married persons have a desire for freedom and a longing to relate to others. This alternative was sought not so much because of marital dissatisfaction, but for the opportunity these extramarital relationships would provide for emotional growth. The solution they propose is to individualize marriage in order to provide equal freedom to grow inside and outside the marriage, to encourage separate growth experiences, to drop the pretense of a couple front, and to develop nonexclusive attitudes toward each other.

These somewhat revolutionary ideas about alternative marriage styles are taken very seriously by the youth culture; and we think they deserve thoughtful consideration and examination as a valid alternative to monogamous marriage for at least some people. For ourselves, we are skeptical that the primary partners in such an alternative arrangement can really develop a mutually cooperative and collaborative exploring relationship that grows ever deeper and richer during the years of living together. We wonder, moreover, whether "open marriage" can honestly deliver the gift of sureness and security about the self-role and the role of the spouse. A loving person in the marital relationship transcends superficial difference and petty selfishness, and tolerates some frustration of individual needs and wishes by giving himself or herself honestly, openly, and fully to the other.

"Loving" another person means placing the welfare and happiness of that person preeminently in one's own thought and actions. The bigamist, polygamist, or synergamist can give only a part of himself (or herself) to each partner, no matter how loving he tries to be in his actions toward all of them. We suspect as well that the full development of each person's potential is stunted in group marriages because there is less need to resolve ambivalences and individual hang-ups.

Consider, for example, two women in a group marriage, one more "maternal" and the other more "sexy." The man will almost invariably prefer one for a coital partner and the other for support and nurturance. He will have less interest therefore in helping each "wife" develop into a more complete woman, capable of a variety of female roles. The converse of these relationships shows the same pattern.

And what of the man or woman who needs to develop the capacity to love? With many people there is less pressure to be a loving person because they can depend on others to solve the partner's problem of loneliness, need for affection, and support. The initial excitement and adventure of new people, who are at first more fantasy than real people, is dampened by the intimate knowledge that comes with time and experience through living with them. Eventually "new people" become simply "people," with their own gifts and limitations. The drive to adjust, to make the compromises that every intimate living situation requires, will become progressively more painful, and in the end, account for the rather frequent failure of such experiences. Competition to be preferred and valued above others will also be a serious problem. When you value and love a person above all others, you do not really want to share that person with another.

ANTISEXUALISM

It deserves noting that not all of the newly promulgated sexual behavior is open and permissive. A wave of antisexualism has rippled through extremist groups of the women's liberation movement and attacks men for treating women as venereal objects in what is described as a "sexist society." Beauty contests, the use of the sexual sell in advertising, and prostitution are all seen as evidence of male chauvinist depersonalization of women into sex objects. But, more to the point of this discussion, some of these groups demand abolition of marriage on the grounds that it is demeaning and degrading to women by restricting them to second-class citizenship. Some have gone so far as to form leagues of young women (now more prominent in Great Britian than the United States) who want to be free to be mothers without the burden of wifery.

The horror and repugnance which the new feminists see in marital sexuality derives from a false equation of the female sexual role with passivity and submission. This notion has led (erroneously, albeit logically) to a self-picture of inferiority. We think this view of the female sexual role mistaken, and that a more accurate term to describe the feminine sexual role is "receptivity" – a term which implies that the female actively and appropriately collaborates in *all* the actions which express a shared love. The receptive role is an aggressive, assertive stance which claims a share of the responsibility for mating.

The myth of the vaginal orgasm has also provoked feelings of inadequacy in many women. In recent years women's sexual responsiveness to stimulation has been carefully investigated by Masters and Johnson (6), and their studies should finally lay to rest the controversial and damaging theory that vaginal orgasms are the only true orgasms for women.

Much of the confusion and misunderstanding between men and women about sexuality results from ignorance about qualitative differences in sexual arousal. We know now that women depend more on context and understanding to become sexually stimulated, and that men are definitely more visually oriented. Positive appreciation of these differences should contribute to mutual understanding and more complementary cooperative relationships between men and women.

CHILDLESS MARRIAGES

Many of our young people now plan to bear no children. They argue that we must limit parenthood to small numbers of families in order merely to replenish our numbers of people; and their goal (shared by many older people) is zero population growth. Moreover, they take seriously the dire ecological consequences of overpopulation which include ever more critical shortages in food supply and distribution all over the world. In addition, they cite the socially disruptive effects triggered by high population density which behavioral scientists do, in fact, observe (17): that circumstances of overcrowding make social relations more superficial, anonymous, and transitory; that human contact may be discouraged and extend even to refusal to become involved in the emergency needs of another person. Furthermore, public health officials note that the incidence of mental illness, drug abuse, and violence is highest in the most overcrowded areas.

All of these are legitimate reasons for concern about overpopulation; and to the extent that young people take an interest in this problem, and make mature choices to do something personally about it, they should be applauded. We suspect, however, that some of the reasons are a thinly veiled exemption from parenthood.

Intellectualism is a principal architect of discontent with the parental role. An overvaluation of the superiority of mind cultivation, abstract thinking, and theorizing leads to devaluation of such important tasks as child rearing. There is sound evidence, moreover, that many young people wish to prolong indefinitely their adolescent state owing to fear of the intimacy, commitment, and responsibility which parenthood implies.

This is not to suggest that a responsible decision for unparenthood cannot be made. Indeed the religious ethics of western culture, together with our current social customs, allows this choice because we know that decisions of this sort finally reside deep within those who are most immediately affected by them, the couple themselves. Persons are surely free not to have children, although in doing so they also forego a fulfillment which no other experience provides.

If we can begin to overcome those rooted traditions in our history which locate our humanity in a faculty or substance, we may likewise begin to understand that we do not *have* sexuality in the sense that it is a possession to be kept or discarded. Whether to be a sexual creature is not an option for us; how we will use our sexuality to express ourselves is among the weighty decisions we make. We *are* sexual beings, and our sexuality is at least one of the ways in which we relate to each other at both superficial and profound levels of experience. So we cannot any longer suppose that our sexuality is merely a function of metabolism. It is that, of course, but it is also a means and an end for communicating ourselves.

Plants and animals express their sexuality, so far as we know, as merely natural phenomena; that is, they "throw off," as it were, objective evidence of themselves through sexual reproduction. But there is at least this much difference between the sexual activity of plants and animals and that of persons: persons procreate other unique, never-to-be-repeated persons. Persons enflesh themselves; and that is why the sexual union of men and women is never a matter of simple reproduction or recreation but always an evidence, when it is authentic, of a loving relationship between them.

Human sexuality, then, is relationship — it engenders and establishes, or destroys and ruptures, community between us. Our sexuality certainly employs those organs and systems commonly (but mistakenly if this is all that is meant) called reproductive. But these organs and systems also, and perhaps more importantly, perform a service for us by functioning to express who we are in relationship. Thus, words like marriage, rape, adultery, and the like take on human and personal meaning because they signify a relationship between persons, which is the clue to the meaning of these actions. Teenagers, together with the rest of us, need to acknowledge that our bodies are the instruments of our self-expression.

TEENAGE MARRIAGE

The size of the married teenage population is impressive (18): eleven percent of women, aged 15 to 19, are married; conversely, only four percent of men, aged 15 to 19, are married. This figure for men is a small percentage, but with our considerable population, it still constitutes a sizeable number (over 250,000). Additionally, while it is impossible to quote exact figures, numerous studies (19, 20) suggest that a majority of teenage brides are pregnant. Approximately fifty percent of early marriages end in divorce. These divorces, tragic enough for the couples, are even more severe if the teenage couple has children.

Young couples themselves are under considerable stress; and LaBarre has suggested that teenage couples who are facing parenthood are also exposed simultaneously to three critical crises (21). They are still in adolescent crisis, not having yet completed the psychologic process of constructing a mature self-concept. Yet, they are expected to develop and maintain the intimate, mutual, collaborative, dyadic relationship of husband and wife. This alone is an exceedingly difficult task, and it is compounded for any person who is still uncertain of self-identity and lacking clear direction in life. In addition, the young couple faces daily the wife's continuing pregnancy and imminent parenthood. LaBarre (22) emphatically states that society has not demonstrated sufficient interest in these young couples. Many school systems consider pregnancy and/or marriage among their students to be ample reason to require their exclusion from the secondary school.

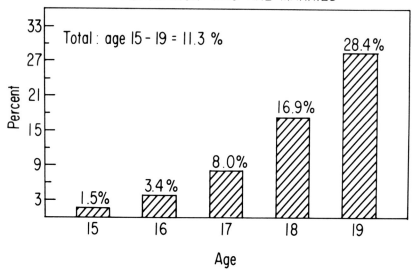

Figure 8. Married teenage population based on information from 1970 census.

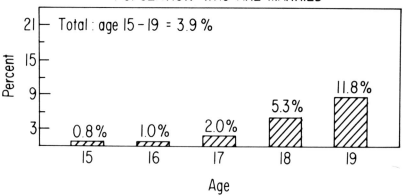

Figure 9. Married teenage population based on information from 1970 census.

Thus the couple is further burdened with limited educational opportunities in a society which usually gives the good jobs to the well educated.

Salutory efforts on the part of a number of states to provide adequate educational services for pregnant and/or married teen-agers are as yet insufficient. Meantime, since jobs for untrained people are so unrewarding and irregular, most teenage couples must rely upon their parents to provide economic assistance. And misguided parents, in turn, often use the fact of their economic assistance to interfere in the couple's decision-making. To make matters worse, the young husband and wife will frequently align with their respective parents against each other. In a study of young married women, Powell (23) noted that young wives, in particular, complain bitterly about parental interference and their husbands' tendencies to side with their own mothers during such power struggles.

Many have stated that sexual relations are not a problem; yet LaBarre (24) reported that only one of ten girls in her study indicated satisfactory sexual relations. Powell (23) reported that young wives did indeed complain about their husbands' failure to provide affection and understanding, and their tendency to treat sexual relations as only a physical experience. It may well be that a wife's pregnancy is stressful to the husband, who may then emotionally regress to a more childlike dependent state (21).

Teenage males may understandably feel trapped in a situation in which they continuously feel inadequate. They are not able to provide adequate income, housing, or social life; and their wives communicate that they do not provide enough husbandly support. When this is so, it is not surprising that many of these young husbands quickly gravitate back to their previous teenage pursuits. There, among their sex peers, they are treated as equals.

THE UNWED FATHER

The unwed father is an infrequently studied person in our culture. But such studies as there are tend to show that he is often more interested in the girl and their baby than popular sentiment would credit. For the most part, he appears not to be the restless, inner-driven, neurotic person who compulsively impregnates women. Rather he seems to be making a sensible decision – in this case, not to compound one mistake (premature fatherhood) with another (premature husbandhood). Usually these teenage boys are quite willing to help the pregnant girl within the constraints of their means (25).

Chapter Four

HOMOSEXUALITY

GENERAL CONSIDERATIONS

W HAT exactly is meant by the term homosexuality? Is it a state of mind, or a pattern of behavior? Beiber (26) states simply: "A homosexual is one who engages repeatedly, in adult life, in sexual relations with members of the same sex." But Marmour (27) points out that this definition fails to make a distinction between those who indulge in homosexual behavior out of an intense sexual attraction to members of the same sex and those who engage in such behavior for a variety of other reasons (among which are prolonged heterosexual deprivation, money, adventure, curiosity, need to please, hostility, and rebellion). Freud (28), as is well known, thought that all human beings went through a homoerotic phase in their development and that arrest due to psychic trauma would cause fixation and homosexual behavior. Even with continuing psychosexual evolution, Freud felt that latent homosexual tendencies would exist, although sublimated, in friendships with members of the same sex.

Homosexuality engenders many points of view, together with considerable confusion and misinformation. It also expresses itself in a variety and diversity of practices. And we need, therefore, to indicate more precisely what the term means. We can begin descriptively.

Common practices between male homosexuals include mutual masturbation (either simultaneously or alternately), fellatio (oral penile intercourse), and anal intercourse. Female homosexuals may practice masturbation, cunnilingus, breast sucking, and simulated genital-to-genital intercourse. Actual sexual practices may be highly varied, and limited only by the imagination and preference of the partners. But it deserves noting that it is not these specific acts as such which are homosexual; indeed, precisely the practices we have enumerated are commonly referred to in marriage manuals as variations for heterosexual couples!

It is the preference for a member of one's own sex as a sexual partner that clinically defines homosexuality; and that choice appears just now to be controlled by psychologic factors. A number of professionals, following the lead of Dr. Kinsey, tend to dismiss the questions of "how" and "why" on the ground that homosexuality, in view of its high incidence, is normal. Kinsey's "statistical normality" − in which he found that approximately thirty-seven percent of American males had some homosexual experience (3) − raised a storm of protest in his day; but more recently his study and conclusions have been criticized (and sometimes discounted) because of his method of sampling and his failure to distinguish between prepuberal and adult homosexual experience.

So interest in the etiology of homosexuality is once again the focus of many investigators. Probably the best study to date is a nine-year analytic study of 106 homosexual and 100 heterosexual males, which was conducted by the research committee of New York City's Society of Medical Psychoanalysts. This work documents that a parental constellation most likely to produce a homosexual son is a detached, hostile father and a close-binding, intimate, seductive mother who is a dominating, minimizing wife. This group was able, by analysis, to produce a change to heterosexual orientation in over one third of their patients (26).

Not all practitioners achieve such a high incidence of change; and few could be as optimistic as Dr. Edmund Bergler (29), who supposedly located the origin of homosexuality in a psychic masochism and wrote that most homosexuals who sincerely desired change could secure it with several years of psychoanalysis. It is true that a substantial number of homosexuals seek treatment for symptoms of depression, anxiety, suicidal impulse, loneliness, and the like; but many of these symptoms can be helped without affecting a fundamental change in sexual partner preference. Instead, patients often learn to choose partners who can better meet their psychological needs because they have developed a more realistic attitude toward their own difficulties.

For example, a male homosexual graduate student, age 25,

suffered profound depression that prevented him from completing his dissertation. Therapy uncovered a hostile, resentful attitude toward his principal advisor; and this, in turn, prevented him from asking for help with his studies. Matters were made worse when the advisor constructively criticized his work, forcing the patient to devote his time to an exaggerated defense of himself. The stoppage of work progress was responsible for the depression. Therapy uncovered a mixup in the patient's mind between his professional advisor and his own hated father; and clarification and separation of the two individuals produced a gratifying progress of academic work together with subsequent disappearance of depressive symptoms. Sexual orientation was unchanged.

Although estimates of the total number of male and female homosexuals in America range from four to ten millions, we do not yet know precisely how or why persons are or become homosexuals. We need to know more about whether the preference for a member of one's own sex as a sexual partner results from socialization processes, biochemical mechanisms, ideological commitments, or some combination of these or other factors. Meanwhile homosexuality is not only a matter of serious medical interest but it is becoming increasingly a matter of public and political discussion.

In the United States, homosexual acts between males are criminal offenses in almost every state, although the nature of the punishment and the type of act punishable vary greatly from state to state. Common terms used legally to describe homosexual acts are "sodomy," and "sexual acts against nature." Moreover, there are other sanctions against homosexuals in our society. The Civil Service Commission refuses to employ homosexuals and may discharge them from employment if they are discovered. Known homosexuals are not allowed military careers, and soldiers discovered committing homosexual acts are discharged as undesirable from the U.S. armed forces.

THE HOMOSEXUAL MOVEMENT

Large segments of American Society look upon homosexuality with disfavor or outright condemnation, and reflect the attitude of an oft-quoted Biblical injunction: "You shall not lie with a male as with a woman, it is an abomination." (Leviticus 18:22) But society's stance, together with the attraction of like-minded company, has produced homosexual subcultures in all of our major cities. Sometimes these homosexual communities are concentrated in residential areas, but most often they are the "gay bars" which serve both social and sexual purposes.

In addition, there are established homophile organizations (e.g., the Mattachine Society and the Daughters of Bellitus) which not only promote social acceptance of homosexuality but also assist homosexuals to find jobs and obtain legal advice. For our generation, the regretable veil of silence in the media that has made frank discussions of homosexuality taboo is slowly lifting. And homosexuals themselves are organizing politically in order to protest, and work for the repeal of, laws and customs they consider discriminatory.

"Gay Liberation," as a concept, holds that a homosexual has a moral right to become, to be, and to remain homosexual; to live his or her homosexuality fully and freely and openly without pressure to convert to heterosexuality; to be free of penalties, disabilities, or disadvantages of any kind — whether public or private, official or unofficial — for his or her nonconformity (30). A persistent theme of Gay Liberation is the rejection of the notion that homosexuality is pathological, or in any sense a symptom of a pathology of any kind. Indeed, some homosexual organizations have adopted formal positions which hold, in substance, that in the absence of valid scientific evidence to the contrary, homosexuality cannot properly be considered a sickness, illness, disturbance, disorder, neurosis, or pathology of any kind. Homosexuality must be properly considered, it is argued instead, as a preference, orientation, or propensity which is not different in kind from heterosexuality and fully equal to it.

Part of the success of the movement to date is reflected in the fact that, although most states have laws prohibiting male homosexuality, the incidence of arrest and prosecution is declining to the point of relative infrequency. And this, together with psychiatric theory which looks upon homosexuality as a block in psychosexual development toward heterosexuality, may explain why psychiatric organizations (which only a few years ago were in the forefront of those groups urging humane consideration for homosexuals) now find themselves being attacked — sometimes violently — by gay liberationists.

FEMALE HOMOSEXUALITY

One of the striking features of our culture's attitudes toward homosexuality is that, when compared with male homosexuality, female homosexuality is not only less politically active but also (maybe because?) more neglected as a subject of clinical investigation and considerably less disfavored in the public mind. Two women live together without arousing gossip or the ire of neighbors, and female homosexuality is virtually never prosecuted by law. Among the obvious reasons which contribute to this circumstance, two notions deserve citing: this is still largely a man's world and the tacit inferiority of women makes what they do together or with each other not very important; and, secondly, the large majority of those who write on homosexuality are (like ourselves!) men who (unlike ourselves!) entirely restrict their investigations to male homosexuality, either because of some pro-male sexual curiosity or perhaps because the thought that some women do not prefer men as sexual partners is unpleasant and repugnant and thus worthy of ignoring.

A more substantive reason for the general neglect of female homosexuality is that relationships between women more nearly resemble normal heterosexual relationships. Tenderness, caring for each other, being considerate of each other appear to be just as important — if not more important — to women than explicit venereal relationships. This close resemblance to heterosexual patterns in female homosexual relationships contrasts sharply with usual male homosexual behavior which heavily emphasizes the venereal aspects of sex, is frequently promiscuous, and sometimes tends to exploit partners with little or no apparent concern for other needs than those immediately related to orgasmic gratification.

Sympathetic plays and movies tend to portray the fiction that male homosexual relationships are just like heterosexual ones.

Perhaps. But our experience is that male homosexual pairs who are deeply involved with each other are rare; indeed, psychiatrists do not usually see such people. Nevertheless, many of our finest contemporary artists either claim, or are said to be homosexuals and promulgate a homosexual outlook in sometimes direct — and sometimes surreptitious — forms. In these works marriage is depicted as unhappy, difficult, tiresome, boring; men and women are portrayed as natural enemies; and heterosexuality is cast as a parody of homosexuality with increasing emphasis on frequent change of partners, casual sex, and group sex.

THE RIGHT TO PRIVACY

Certainly many educated people have taken the tolerant attitude that, regardless of their own personal feelings, sexual relations between consenting adults in private is their own business. But legalization need not be confused with sanction or approval. It is surely arguable that homosexuals should be treated with care and respect; but to glorify their style of life as equal to, and at times superior to, the heterosexual style, ordinarily contradicts what we know to be sound and healthy about human relationships.

Unfortunately the claims that homosexuality is the exclusive province of homosexuals and that homosexuality is normal, overlook possible damage which these kinds of statements can engender. Homosexuals, who are reassured that their homosexuality is normal, may fail to seek treatment which might alter their life style orientation to a heterosexual one. This kind of thinking may also profoundly affect the young and immature who are looking for an outlet for their sexual tensions. In short, not only has the homosexual a stake in what society's attitudes towards homosexuals are, but society itself has an important stake.

ADOLESCENT HOMOSEXUALITY

Since adolescence is the usual age when erotic strivings are awakened and people realize they are making emotional attachments to persons of the same sex, it seems desirable that physicians (or other adults who serve as counselors and who might be called upon to intervene) understand as much about homosexuality as our best information now indicates.

Studies of homosexuals point out that most of them have their first homosexual experience during their early teens. In fact a large proportion have already "come out" (a term which signals emergence into gay society) by the time they are in their late teens. The acceptance of their homosexuality by the subculture group does much to deter their feelings of shame or guilt.

The period prior to "coming out" is often a time of intense emotional turmoil as the adolescent struggles to develop a sexual identity. The high rate of suicide in homosexual adolescent males in particular is an indicator of this turmoil. Unfortunately, due to society's negative attitude toward homosexuality, there are very few places for such young people to go where they can discuss their feelings and experiences.

Development of a homosexual self-concept takes time. In addition it is frought with real physical hazards. There are many dangerous individuals who prey on homosexuals, sometimes even killing them in sadistic orgies. The young and inexperienced are common victims of such people.

Teenage homosexuals — particularly handsome, slim youths — are considered to be very desirable sexual partners and are much sought after in the homosexual world where searching for fresh "talent" is a consuming passion. Many such youths quickly gravitate into dependent relationships with older men who may use gifts, promises of jobs, and other inducements to court their favor. Some may give up all other pursuits and accept a courtesan-like career until their "good looks" fade. Much like the aging glamour girl, when their desirability diminishes they have no personal resources to fall back upon. Just as in the heterosexual world, homosexual relationships built upon mere physical attraction do not endure.

Similarly, teenage homosexual girls often gravitate into relationships with older women who seduce them by gratifying their intense dependency strivings. Oftentimes such relationships will be highly emotional, particularly on the part of the younger women. In such an atmosphere "cheating" or "break-ups" may

Figure 10. Door decoration of seventeen-year-old homosexual youth who was admitted following serious suicidal attempt.

precipitate drinking episodes, suicidal attempts, or even assaults. Many homosexual women hate men because they are thought to be rivals in the pursuit of young girls.

Teenage homosexual girls often date boys and may even, in a limited way, enjoy their company. They frequently gravitate to homosexual boys whom they see as "safe." At times these young girls are sought after by older married couples. Usually the older woman has homosexual interests which her husband tolerates. Often the girl meets special emotional needs of the wife, which the husband cannot allow, to dominate another person. In such cases the husband is really bait, offering the girl security and protection in exchange for becoming the passive and compliant companion of the wife.

THERAPY

Parents' reaction to their teenagers' homosexuality varies from violent outrage to calm acceptance. Unfortunately, some parents view this homosexual behavior as a personal afront to their own child rearing diligence. Their ego is wounded. They become defensive, harsh, and bitter. They bring the teenager to a therapist hoping that he can effect a changed sexual orientation. Teenagers, not surprisingly, view the therapist as the parent's agent who is not to be trusted. Moreover, their own self-esteem has been severely lowered as a result of feeling out of step with society and parents. Some teenagers adopt an arrogant, condescending, superior stance which is very difficult to accept. The usual helping, supporting, "let me take care of you," "rely on me" attitude of the physician only serves to increase the teenagers' fear and defiance; and they stay aloof and suspicious.

How does one help such patients? Acceding to their fears by withdrawing from a therapeutic role may give teenagers momentary relief but may increase their isolation, which can get so unbearable as to precipitate a suicidal act. Withdrawal also serves to confirm their conviction that adult or "straight" contacts hold no rewards for them.

The answer lies in permitting teenagers to maintain the distance their fears demand but not to get provoked into total rejection of the patient. The tactful therapist must be able to empathize with the patient's problems. Treatment progress can be made only after a successful relationship has been established. Even with a well-motivated patient, a change in sexual orientation is possible in only fifty percent of cases. Far more important than change is to help repair the patient's damaged self-esteem.

As is evident thus far, homosexual relationships are diverse, running the gamut from the most furtive, strictly sexual encounter between strangers to intense, complex, polygamous affairs. Sorting out these myriad relationships and helping patients understand their meaning and purpose often permits them to make wiser choices about the people with whom they choose to associate.

CONCLUSIONS

There is, of course, nothing new about homosexuality. It was well known to the cultures of Greece (where homosexuality was accepted) and Rome (where it was tolerated). The Bible (e.g. Genesis 19:1-28) makes it plain that homosexuality was abhorrent to the Israelites; and later Rabbinic commentary strengthened that attitude by providing cruel penalties for sodomy. It can be fairly said that subsequent Judeo-Christian attitudes are little more than refinement of the ancient Israelite position; and Western Culture has followed that lead by stamping homosexuality as taboo and providing extensive legal sanctions.

We do not yet know why persons are or become homosexuals. There is increasing data which suggest that society, through repressive sexual attitudes and persecution of social deviates, supports the development of this sexual subculture. And it is no secret that American prisons are spawning grounds for homosexuals; indeed, the Institute for Sex Research estimates that seventy percent of all long-term prisoners become practicing homosexuals.

While there is some controversy over whether the term homosexuality is so perjorative as to be excluded from the psychiatric diagnostic manual, we think it fair to state that the large majority of American psychiatrists clearly accept hetero-sexuality as the model of authentic human sexual relationships. We do not exclude ourselves from this group. On the other hand, we do acknowledge, in the words of the Wolfenden Report (31), that "there must remain a realm of private morality and immorality which is, in brief and crude terms, not the law's business." More importantly, as counselors we cannot reject homosexuals who come to us seeking help. Understanding, sympathy, and assistance seem to us unarguably more appropriate responses than antagonism, vilification, and punishment.

Chapter Five

THE PROMISCUOUS TEENAGER

THE promiscuous adolescent girl is a source of much concern to her parents, is held in relatively low esteem by peers, and frequently confronts the physician with problems in management.

While it is true that, among our young today, premarital sex standards have undergone relaxation, today's youth continue (for the most part) to reject casual, indiscriminate, or promiscuous sexuality. In a relatively thorough study by Zelnik and Kanter (1), twenty-eight percent of unmarried girls ages fifteen to nineteen reported that they had had sexual intercourse, but of these, almost half had had no sexual contact within the last month. Of the remaining group who acknowledged sexual contact within the last month, nine out of ten had only one partner.

Today's youth typically court openly with very little chaperoning by adults, and have increasing mobility and access to privacy in cars, apartments, and. hotels. Our society places autonomous decision making in the hands of the young in almost every area of their lives; they are encouraged to choose values which are "right for them." And sex, when it is a part of their lives, usually occurs within the context of a close, affectionate, long lasting relationship. Nevertheless, there exists a group of restless, frequently alienated, rebellious teenagers who compulsively reach out for premature, precocious sexual experience where their partners are strangers or very recent acquaintances, and where no meaningful human relationship with the sex partner is sought.

Understandably such behavior causes parents to become concerned, apprehensive, embarrassed, and angry. Parental attempts to control this behavior by counseling, restricting, and punishing the teenager have almost always met with failure before professional help is sought.

One of the authors is a psychiatric consultant to adolescent patients at a state hospital in eastern North Carolina. This area is predominately agricultural and dotted with small towns. The population of this large area is only 1,400,000; and of the thirty-three counties in the region, only one of them (Onslow) has as many as 100,000 people. The recognition that adolescents need a milieu that provides special educational and therapeutic services led to the development of this unit in 1965. Since that time over five hundred young patients have received services there.

In an effort to strengthen our own approach to the problem of promiscuity, we reviewed the records of twenty psychiatrically disturbed teenage girls who have received residential treatment and who had, as one of their presenting problems, "promiscuous sexual behavior." In none of these cases was promiscuity the sole cause for admission. Other reasons included psychosis, illicit drug usage, school failure, and runaway episodes. Promiscuity was defined as sexual contact with at least three different partners over the preceding year.

THE FAMILY ENVIRONMENT

Familial discord in this group appeared to be very common. In five cases, the mother was the sole parent living in the home and in one case the father reared the girl with the help of his mother. In three cases, the father was a severe alcoholic. In four cases, the current home was intact but the mother, herself, had divorced and remarried at least three times during the daughter's growing years. In the remaining seven cases, the girls were living with their biological parents who had relatively intact marriages. It would be more accurate to say that of these latter seven marriages, five had the appearance of stability. In one, the mother married at age fourteen; in another at age sixteen. In two families, the mothers were very passive, submissive, masochistic women who were dominated by their husbands and children. In another, there was a definite suspicion that the father had placed the daughter in a surrogate wife role and rejected the mother. He was alleged to have shown his daughter pornographic films and to have had sexual relations with her as well. This particular girl was suffering from a schizophrenic disorder. In yet another case, the mother was diagnosed borderline psychotic and was very domineering with the husband and the children. Only the remaining two marriages had marital relationships characterized by warmth, mutuality of interests, and maturity.

THE ROLE OF THE MOTHER

In fifteen of the cases, the marital relationship was severely disrupted. The nature of the disruption would lead one to speculate that the mothers of these girls were in a severe state of marital deprivation. They were not getting from their spouses emotional security and support. These husbands were either absent from the home, alcoholic, domineering, passive, or rejecting. A review of the social worker's recorded interview with the mother confirmed our speculation. For the most part these were unhappy women, often forced to work outside the home, overwhelmed by their responsibilities, and angry at their husbands.

This deprivation state definitely interfered with the mother's providing adequate love and support. In a number of these cases the mother had to place the girl, during her formative years, temporarily in institutions. In the household the relationship with the daughter tended to be distant. The girls were largely left to fend for themselves. They were viewed as a burden. This lack of love and support prevented the daughters from learning to value and cherish themselves as people and as women. Lacking any sense of self-value or self-respect as persons, they were more ready to sell themselves for the things they desperately needed. In most cases this was affection or its substitute (drugs, clothes, money, favors).

For example: D. was an adopted sixteen-year-old white female currently in the tenth grade. The girl previously had been expelled from school for stealing from a teacher's purse. She had already run away on two occasions. On the latest occasion, she had a severe quarrel with her mother over whether she could date a twenty-one-year-old soldier. She ran away and lived for a while with "Chip," with whom she had sexual intercourse and "dropped speed." She explained: "He was giving me drugs and I was paying him back." She was brought to a hospital while on a "bad trip." Her parents were notified and transferred her to the state hospital. Eighteen months previously she had run away and supported a forty-dollar-per-day heroin habit by prostitution. She changed boyfriends frequently. The father was described by the social worker as a cold, remote man who was a retired military officer. The mother was described as verbally aggressive and seductive with other men.

MEN AS MATERNAL SUBSTITUTES

The lack of warmth and security which these girls feel at home, and the resultant poor self-concept, often produce a hunger for love and affection which are sought indiscriminately, not only from boys who replace the mother in the girls' nurturent fantasies but from "love substitutes" like drugs, clothes, cosmetics, and the like. This hunger impairs their judgment and frequently places them in real danger from potentially sadistic partners.

C. was a frequent runaway, who was admitted after she was picked up by police and noted to have "pot" and "speed" in her possession. During these runaway trips, she would stay with and sleep with any man who came along. On one occasion she was secluded for a period of time by several soldiers, and on another occasion she stayed with some truck drivers who picked her up on the road. Her runaway episodes were usually precipitated by a quarrel with her mother. She had a history of maternal neglect. The mother's first two marriages were to alcoholics. The present marriage was to a man who had little or no use for C., and at one time refused to have her live in his home. C. had been placed in homes for juveniles during her early years. On admission, C. was an easy going, slow talking, rather apathetic youngster. She was dressed like the "flower child" she was. She admitted readily to taking speed and seemed oblivious to staff warnings about the dire consequences of this drug. On one occasion, she was apprehended performing fellatio on another teenager in whom she was only casually interested. She was a compulsive shoplifter, who stole clothing and cosmetics. She appeared not to care what happened to her, had little ambition, and showed no interest in her school work.

Relations between mother and daughter were so strained that the mother refused to take C. home for Christmas, despite evidence of improvement during the previous two months. Fortunately, with time and counseling, her relationship with her mother improved. She had several productive home visits. The father started taking more interest in her and she was discharged to home with an appointment at her local mental health center.

This type of search for nurturance from men is further, and graphically, detailed in an "obscene letter" by a highly intelligent thirteen-year-old patient to a male patient. The following are excerpts:

> My dearest love, HI!!
>
> What's happening besides you? As far as I'm concerned you're always what's happening anywhere you are or wherever you go! Honey, I think we could make it together *only* and *only* if we went somewhere where nobody knows you! If we lived together I could eat you all I wanted to and you could do likewise. Mostly, we could fuck all the time. Well, Love! I really should split for now, so I'll see you Wednesday night at the dance.
>
> > Love always,
> > (Your girl, I hope) C.

The coldness and rejection the teenager feels from the mother exaggerates the normal antagonisms and hostilities between the generations. Adolescent rebelliousness, typical of most teenagers, is not tempered in these cases by loving positive feelings between the participants. In these circumstances only permissive attitudes from the mother are tolerated. Any attempt to set even reasonable limits is seen as an intolerable abridgment of freedom and is equated with lack of love. This sets the stage for an all-out war on mother, her stated values and expectations. Winning over mother becomes "the only thing."

P. was a seventeen-year-old white female who previously had been hospitalized at a university hospital. On admission, she acted tough and arrogant and spouted psychological jargon that she had learned from her previous contact with psychiatry. She was involved in a bitter conflict with her mother who was a harsh, domineering, and bad tempered person. The father was a quiet, passive man. The family lived in a small, southern town; and P.

was promiscuous, but only with black teenagers. This dating pattern represented a direct assault on her mother and her family's values. In reality, she took little interest in these youngsters as human beings but would entice them, use them as bludgeons against her parents for a short time, and then drop them. She had an IQ of 120, but her school work was poor. Her admission was precipitated by an episode of running away.

An occasional mother seems covertly to encourage her daughter's promiscuity. Apparently in these cases, the erotic needs of the mother are vicariously gratified by the teenager's behavior (32). For example: K. was a fourteen-year-old white girl who was the youngest of three children. The mother was a lonely, insecure woman; and the father was a sporadic alcoholic whose job kept him away from the family during the week. K's mother, who was very permissive, could not set realistic limits on K's dating. Instead, when K. would return late at night from one of her sexual foraging operations, the mother would want to know what had happened. She would question K., and then nag and criticize her for her behavior. Overtly, her mother disapproved of K's behavior; but her total lack of determination and discipline in dealing with K. betokened the opposite. K. had been sexually active, compulsively pursuing boys, since the age of ten (the time of menarche). In the hospital, she had tried to seduce the male visitors of other patients, and was in constant "hot water" with the other girls for her predatory behavior. She was admitted to the hospital when her school truancy brought her to the attention of authorities, who demanded that something be done. The mother reluctantly consented; and almost from the start of K's residential treatment, she pleaded with the staff to let K. come home on weekends so she could be with her family. (Actually, K. spent weekends with her sexual partners.)

Most of these girls had poor relations with other girls. They aggressively pursued boys, often attempting to seduce even the male visitors of other female patients. Since they changed boyfriends frequently, and seemingly capriciously, they often provoked fights among jealous boyfriends.

PSYCHOLOGICAL TESTING

Psychologic testing, particularly projective techniques, usually confirms the impression that these girls perceive their mothers as cold and rejecting and the fathers as distant or seductive. The Minnesota Multiphasic Personality Inventory often shows elevation in scales 4 (PD) and 9 (MA) (see fig. 11). These scales measure, among other traits, psychopathic trends and tendencies to act impulsively.

Most of the girls had average to slightly above average IQ's. Only a few had IQ's in the border-line mental retardation range. A large proportion had an educational deficiency, as manifested by a reading level several grades behind what one would expect for their age and IQ. Of those who were already out of school, none had any vocational training in preparation for employment prior to their admission.

Emphasis has long been placed on the early formative years as crucial for the successful resolution of the adolescent struggle for a secure self-concept. Thus, Dr. Bingham Dai (15) states:

> Child rearing methods and ethical principles by themselves may be of little avail unless parents, themselves, and those having direct dealings with the child have achieved self-concepts of such a kind that they will not wittingly or unwittingly utilize their relations with the child mainly for the gratification of their own private needs. Only in this manner can they genuinely and consistently love and respect the child as an individual, and only in this manner can the child in turn learn to love and respect himself as a human being and eventually acquire the kind of adequate growth facilitating primary self which seems to be the only true foundation of mental health.

The results of hospital treatment varied. In the forty percent of cases in which ameriolation of promiscuous behavior was most successful, two factors were evident: (1) we had established a good working relationship with the mother who was able to vent her pent-up rage and discouragement, not only about her daughter but her own life. From there, with the help of the staff, she was able to be more genuine and consistent in loving her daughter as a person. Such matters as setting limits were handled better. (2) The girl herself acquired a more positive attitude toward herself as a

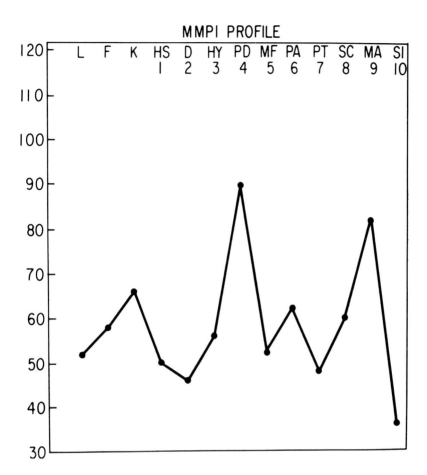

Figure 11. MMPI of promiscuous teenage girl.

person. Apparently, this was accomplished by developing a good relationship with a mature female staff member, who often became a mother surrogate to the patient. The positive attitude which developed toward this person, and the desire to be like her, appeared to be a significant help in developing respect in and for herself as a human being.

We know that caution must be exercised in generalizing these findings in a group of seriously disturbed teenagers to the typical

Figure 12. Wall decoration in room of severely troubled teenage girl. The embracing nude couple on far right of wall, next to word "experience," contrasts sharply with the demure picture headed, "A Picture of Innocense" (sic).

adolescent patient with promiscuous behavior. So we should point out that, in general, our sample overrepresents the poor and the rural population of North Carolina.

PROMISCUOUS BOYS

Probably we state the obvious when we say that every promiscuous girl has a partner, often another teenager. Contrary to the attitudes ordinarily taken toward girls, the sexual behavior of promiscuous boys is usually of little concern to their parents, often they are held in high esteem by their male peers, and rarely do they consult a physician unless they develop a venereal infection. Our society supposes that sexual decision-making is firmly in the hands of the girl, who then must bear the brunt of responsibility for heterosexual encounter. This was forcefully illustrated in the comment made by a young man about his reasons for dating a particularly notorious promiscuous girl, whom he didn't even like: "You know, Doc, a stiff prick doesn't have any conscience."

Customarily, our society does not admonish a young man for sexual intercourse; although society will, of course, severely punish the young man who rapes. (What constitutes legal rape is somewhat beyond our immediate interest here.) The rapist shares many of the same views about women that promiscuous girls have about themselves: His sexual assault represents an attempt to dominate and degrade the girl, she is useful only for satisfying his need of the moment, and employs his sexual organs to show dominance and ascendency. The following description of sexual activities, by a young rapist, will illustrate:

> They want it — I know they do — they just want somebody to *force them* — they don't *resist* at all most of the time. Now and then you have to *slap* one around a little so that she'll be reasonable. It doesn't take me long. I throw my load and I'm out of there and gone in five minutes.

Some like Kinsey (3), would state that the human male is naturally promiscuous and that only social prohibitions make him monogamous. It is not our purpose here to debate the innate biological predisposition of humans; but it may be appropriate to indicate that some males do behave in a promiscuous fashion *where the goal does not appear to be* the fulfillment of a genuine human need (like love and companionship), or the satisfaction of a curiosity about others, or even simple relief of sexual tension. These boys compulsively seek out one woman after another in a restless and unrelenting pursuit. They appear interested only in conquest; and getting a woman into bed represents victory in the private game they play. Unfortunately, since they are playing games with real people, they can wreak havoc on people's lives. They show little interest in girls as persons and, much like the rapist, use them to satisfy some inner neurotic need.

S. was a young university student from a small town in North Carolina. Since his divorce at age eighteen, he had been playing the field. He attracted a bevy of pretty but somewhat maternal and masochistic coeds. He had artistic interests which disgusted his father, who was a former football hero. His father clearly favored an older son, who was an engineering major and also already a highly touted athlete. S. had always been keenly aware of his father's disappointment in him, and as a result had an extremely low opinion of his own masculinity. This in turn, provoked intensely competitive attitudes toward other male students. S. had no male friends. At age seventeen, he experienced a short-lived, disastrous marriage to an older woman. From that time onward, his life evolved around a succession of conquests.

One of these occurred when S. was invited to visit a coed in her home. During the wee hours of the morning, when everybody else in the household was asleep, he persuaded her to "prove her love with sex." Thereafter they had intercourse every night. When he returned to school, he inadvertently left a condom, used the night before and full of semen, on the night stand. Predictably the girl's mother found it, and the girl herself was then harshly treated by her parents. S's "carelessness," which wreaked such havoc in that family, had dynamic origins. He secretly wished the girl's parents, particularly the father, to find out that he had possessed their daughter. During a therapy session he complained of their discovery and berated their old-fashioned, angry attitude; but his smug, self-satisfied smile betrayed the opposite.

That same summer, S. had impregnated two sisters in his hometown, both of whom had secured abortions after he refused further involvement. He always found some reason that none of these relationships should endure. In reality, he had little interest in the girls as companions but used them to provoke envy and anger from other men. He was troubled by a recurring dream in which he was dressed in red and running from an enormous bull. This dream revealed two important attitudes in his mental life that drove him to behave so outrageously: the red suit symbolized his provocative, competitive attitude toward other men (taking their daughters); the gigantic bull represented his inflated view of other men's prowess (they were larger, stronger, more fierce) and conversely demonstrated how puny and insignificant he felt in their presence.

Advocates of sexual freedom, who promulgate the doctrine that "whatever you do is okay as long as you don't hurt anyone," have had considerable effect on the sexual habits and attitudes of young people. And there is, correspondingly, no doubt that there has been an increase in casual and indiscriminate sexual activity, particularly among college students.

Annual holiday treks to the beaches, which often attract thousands of students, provide at least for some students an opportunity for sexual adventures. One student related this story to us about his trek to a Florida beach during the Christmas holidays:

> I was real excited about going — you know, there would be plenty of girls from all the eastern schools, and from what I'd heard, it would be pretty easy to find one to do it with. When I got there it was fantastic — I mean there were these girls everywhere and they were letting anybody screw them. I went to this one place where I had to wait in line. When I got in, there were three girls — one in each bedroom — and after one guy came out, you just took his place. When I got in the room, there was this very pretty girl lying on the bed naked. She was mildly drunk, probably from pot, and she smiled and said, "Not another one. You boys are so aggressive." And she lay down on the bed waiting. I took off my pants and I started to climb up. She closed her legs and said, "Say you like me, say you like me first." I said, "Sure, I like you"; and she smiled again and lay back, not resisting any more, and I screwed her fast. It didn't take me long. After I finished I put my pants on and left.

Venereal diseases are a real hazard of such indiscriminate sexual activity. Gonorrhea is now foremost among reported communicable diseases. Almost two million cases — approximately one per one hundred persons — were estimated in 1969; and more than one quarter of all cases are teenagers. This disease is, of course, transmitted exclusively by direct sexual contacts. The usual infection begins abruptly, about two to five days after exposure. Urination becomes painful, very frequent, and there is constant feeling of having to urinate. This is accompanied by a copious, pussy discharge from the penile opening. The organism causing this disease used to be exquisitely sensitive to small doses of penicillin (75,000 units in the 1940's), but now the recommended dosage is sixty-four times higher (4,800,000 units). Other antibiotics (tetracyclines) are now being used. The developed resistence of the organisms is now an established pattern and will no doubt increase.

Many women have had asymptomatic infection but do not even realize that they have had the disease, and are thus carriers of the disease. The Center for Disease Control estimates that there may be as many as 640,000 female carriers in the United States. (This vast reservoir of infection has stimulated emergency action in many public health departments, where there is renewed emphasis on screening and VD education.) In addition to detection, women also need to be advised that the infection migrates back through the uterus and into the fallopian tubes (endometritis), and that scarred and damaged tubes are subsequently sometimes incapable of transporting the ova, thereby rendering the woman sterile (33, 34).

While not the most statistically prominent, syphilis is the most serious venereal disease. After contact with an infected person, several months may elapse before a noticeable sign appears. This is usually a painless sore (chancre). Untreated, this primary lesion will disappear, but the disease continues to spread through all parts of the body. After several months, a generalized rash or multiple sores in the mouth may appear. If this symptom is also untreated, the disease then tends to lie quiescent for several years, only to erupt again and attack such vital organs as the heart (causing rupture of an artery or damage to heart valves) or the brain (causing insanity and/or paralysis). Infants born to syphilitic mothers (congenital syphilis) may be sick at birth or develop lesions later. Untreated congenital syphilis can cause blindness, insanity or deformities.

Indeed the consequences of untreated venereal disease are so serious that several states have enacted laws* which permit

*Law of Maryland, Chap. 468, Sec. 1
Massachusetts General Law, Chap. 1, Sec. 117
Nebraska Legislative Bill, No. 280-2
Connecticut, Public Act No. 206

physicians to examine and treat teenagers for venereal infection *without the consent of parents or guardians.* The Maryland law, in particular, extends this concept to include the examination and treatment of unwed pregnant teenagers without either parental consent or disclosure. In these states which have adopted these laws, the way is now open for physicians to intercede medically in cases in which teenagers cannot bring themselves to confide their situation to parents.

Many physicians, together with others, would contend that such laws constitute an abrogation of parental authority and privilege; and, moreover, that these laws run roughshod over fundamental parental rights to advise and consent on matters affecting their children's medical care. At issue also is the serious question of whether a minor (as legally defined) can truly give valid consent to treatment. One might argue further that teenagers, who are so frightened over their situation that they cannot bring themselves even to discuss the matter with parents, are hardly in a position to make such complex and far-reaching decisions alone.

Our purpose here is not to debate the merits of these laws; but we do wish to underscore the seriousness of medical intervention among the young — particularly in view of these serious sexual problems — and the necessity for realistic treatment alternatives for venereal disease and unwanted pregnancy among teenagers.

SUMMARY

The point deserves stressing that promiscuous teenagers are not "bad" kids, or "rotten" children, or any of the other moralizing epithets which so often label them. They are disturbed youngsters who have personal problems which are ordinarily the result of poor family and peer relationships. Their rebelliousness and precocious sexual activity are symptoms of an underlying distress which is rooted in the absence (or deprivation) of self-value. Lacking acceptance and security in conventional relationships, they develop a poor self-concept and indiscriminately seek affirming and bonding associations. The purpose of counseling these teenagers is to facilitate the emergence and growth of the primary self by developing a positive environment; which usually means helping the teenager to establish a comfortable and confident self-concept and assisting parents and child together to cultivate a mutually affirming and supportive alliance.

Chapter Six

ALTERNATIVES TO PARENTHOOD

PROBLEM PREGNANCIES

Teenage pregnancy is an increasingly common occurrence because of the rising numbers of sexually active teenagers. The young people whom we have interviewed with problem pregnancies have, almost without exception, been adequately informed about the "facts of life." Indeed they are often relatively sophisticated youngsters and quite knowledgeable about contraceptives. Some of them have even been successful users of contraceptives in the past who, suddenly and for no readily apparent reason, stopped taking even the most rudimentary precautions and became pregnant.

For some of the young girls we studied, becoming pregnant served a rebellious and hostile purpose toward parents whom they thought overly repressive. Struggles between these girls and their parents were ordinarily over the issue of control and obedience; and frequently there was a marked breakdown in communication together with a feeling of estrangement on the part of the girl. Sexual intercourse was usually explicitly warned against by the parents. The rage and even filicidal impulses some of the parents expressed is an indication of just how deeply the girl's behavior had wounded them. In such cases, the boy is commonly not told of the girl's pregnancy and often discarded. These girls are really little interested in the boys themselves but entice them, use them to bludgeon their parents, and then drop them.

Becoming pregnant does, however, sometime represent an attempt to force marriage upon an unwilling male. These young girls are usually dependent, unhappy persons who blame their parents for their loneliness and isolation. They seek to escape their home and often go to another protected environment where they will be loved and cared for. The young man of their fantasies

73

The Promiscuous Teenager

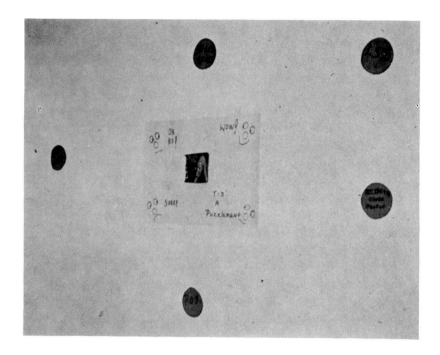

Figure 13. Wall decoration: circle to far right contains words "Accidents cause people," circle to far left contains words "boy hunt."

becomes a suitable vehicle to spirit them away from the hated hearth. Secondarily, pregnancy justifies and rationalizes their craving for protection and succor. Temporarily they are happy, but reality eventually intervenes. The young man is often too immature to meet even legitimate needs (22). He cannot, of course, replace the mother. And, in any event, merely doing his duty is no basis for an acceptable marital arrangement.

Pregnancy for some deeply infatuated young girls can also function to express more love than intercourse alone. Loving the young man means wanting to have his baby. The child is conceived, both mentally and biologically, as her gift to him; and carrying the baby to term and delivery represents her seal of commitment and love.

At the other side, some teenage boys urgently wish to

impregnate a girl to prove their masculinity; and the pregnant girl, in turn, temporarily reaffirms the boy's inadequate sense of maleness. One such young man told us that "screwing with a safety (condom) is like going swimming wearing a raincoat." This was his rationalization for the pregnancy he caused. These boys usually care very little for the girl, and once the event occurs they offer no help. Other young men have confessed to us that they like "taking chances." The sexual act becomes more exciting when one of the possible endpoints can be construed as dangerous.

THE PREGNANT STATE

The initial psychological reaction of teenage girls to pregnancy is sometimes denial: they refuse to accept cessation of menses, tender nipples, nausea, and growing girth as signs of pregnancy. This can be medically dangerous to them, particularly since the medical problems of the pregnant teenager are almost always more severe then those of older women. Teenage girls are susceptible to a higher incidence of hypertension and frequent uterine inertia; and hence more operative deliveries. Denial may also result in delayed abortion which becomes a much more serious procedure after the first trimester of pregnancy. At times the continuation of the pregnancy may have a contingent value to the girl. It may serve to reunite the girl with her mother, and the girl's maternal care and affection can be a meaningful maturing experience.

In order to help the girl, we need some understanding of the reason(s) for the pregnancy, her sense of personal worth, her degree of loneliness and isolation, her family relations and, if possible, the attitude of the young man. The problem of guilt over abortion should also be examined. Only then can the physician be prepared to advise the girl and assist her in her decision about abortion or term delivery.

Since in so many of these cases the pregnancy serves a neurotic, unrealistic need that cannot be met; and since birth out of wedlock is generally unacceptable in our culture, abortion is a frequently sought-after solution. But abortion seldom, if ever, solves these kinds of problems.

ABORTION

In less than two decades, attitudes toward abortion have changed dramatically. Currently, according to a survey by the congressionally chartered Commission on Population Growth and the American Future, half the public favors liberalization of restrictions on abortion. As recently as 1968, however, eighty-five percent of the public opposed more liberal abortion policies.

More than a decade ago, it was estimated that the number of illegally induced abortions annually performed in the United States ranged between 200,000 and 1,200,000. More recently, reliable estimates put the total number of U.S. abortions at about one million, of which ninety-nine percent were estimated to be illegal. Between five hundred and one thousand deaths annually were attributed to illegal abortions; and thousands of other women suffered irreparable mutilations.

The operation itself is now usually quite safe for the woman if performed in the hospital and during the first twenty-four weeks of pregnancy. Until the twelfth week, the standard procedure for abortion has been dilation and curettage (usually abbreviated "D & C"). Using this technique, the surgeon stretches open the cervix, the narrow lower end of the uterus, and removes the conceptus with a scoop-shaped instrument called a curette. More recently, vacuum aspiration of the conceptus has been increasingly employed in both this country and Great Britain. This latter technique is thought to be both more effective and less traumatic to the uterine lining, resulting in fewer complications such as bleeding and uterine perforation.

Extensive studies (35) now tend to show that the mortality and morbidity rates of induced abortion, when performed at an early stage by a trained physician in an adequately equipped hospital or clinic, are relatively low. Indeed, some physicians now regard abortion by D & C or vacuum aspiration as such a benign procedure that the operation is performed in an outpatient clinic (euphemistically called "pregnancy interruption service") without overnight hospitalization. Abdominal or vaginal hysterotomy can result in more serious complications, and these procedures are ordinarily not employed for evacuation of a uterus prior to three months of gravidity. More dangerous and traumatic still is "salting," or deposition of a necrotizing chemical into the amniotic sac, in order to induce labor and evacuate the conceptus *per vaginam.*

Liberalization of abortion laws demonstrates that attitudes toward abortion have changed in American society. The proportion of abortions performed legally for psychiatric reasons has also increased dramatically in recent years, and led some to say that psychiatrists have a greater stake in the clarification of this issue since they are often called upon to render a judgment that society itself has been reluctant to make. Those psychiatrists who go to the literature will receive little help from published reports, because it is very difficult clinically to be certain whether an abortion will alleviate or exacerbate a psychiatric state (there are many threatened, and a few actual, suicides during unwanted pregnancy) (36). Some investigators, like Pfeiffer (37), have pointed out that psychiatrists are increasingly being called upon to justify abortion. When this is so, it tends to be demeaning and degrading to women in the measure to which it encourages them to feign symptoms, mouth suicidal ideas, or argue that women are the "owners" of fetuses and thereby entitled to "abortion on demand" (9).

Advocacy of this latter point of view raises several interesting questions, some of which are especially pertinent to medicine as a profession: is the woman unrestrictedly in charge of her life? Does she have the unchallenged right to determine the destiny of an embryo? Are there competing rights – perhaps of the fetus, the husband or lover, or society – which, in our culture, moderate such plenary and unilateral claims?

Some proponents of abortion on demand point out, as did Robert O. Egberg when he was Assistant Secretary of Health and Scientific Affairs, that abortion is necessary to retard population growth. Others instance the damage of bringing into the world an unwanted child, and cite studies which compare children born after the mother was refused an abortion with a similarly numbered group of wanted children. These studies tend to show poor mental health, poor social adjustment, and lower educational levels among the "unwanted" children. Still others point out that since women are going to secure abortions anyway, and since the morbidity and mortality from criminal abortions is so high, making abortion legally available is the only humane thing to do.

New York was the first state to enact an abortion law which left the decision to the woman and her physician within the first twenty-four weeks of pregnancy. That law took effect July 1, 1970; and New York's experience, which many interpreted as a trial for the rest of the country, was closely observed. During the first year 165,000 abortions were performed — sixty-four percent of them on women from other states and countries. Indeed, abortions became so frequent in New York that the ratio was 950 abortions for every 1,000 live births. Nevertheless, the medical complication rate was only ten per 1000 abortions. Eight mortalities were reported in the first year (38) (probably fewer than the number who would have died if these pregnancies had continued to delivery). It is further interesting to note that Blacks and Puerto Ricans, who had previously little access to legal abortions, received half the abortions done on New Yorkers. In addition, there appeared to be a precipitous decline in the number of illegal abortions; and the maternal mortality rate, to which criminal abortions have always contributed a major portion, reached a record low of 2.3 per 10,000 live births in comparison with 5.2 per 10,000 live births in the previous year (38).

In January, 1973, the United States Supreme Court, in response to cases from Georgia and Texas, overruled all state laws which prohibit or restrict a woman's right to obtain an abortion during the first trimester of pregnancy. That decision also provided that "from and after this point (i.e., the end of the first trimester), a state may regulate the abortion procedure to the extent that the regulation reasonably relates to the preservation and protection of maternal health." The Court held, moreover, that "if the state is interested in protecting fetal life after viability (which the Court defined as the last ten weeks of pregnancy), it may go so far as to prescribe abortion during that period except when it is necessary to preserve the life or health of the mother" (39, 40). That appears to be, just now, where we are as a society.

Is this then the long-awaited solution to the problem pregnancy? Or has there been euphoric emphasis on abortion as a social and economic solution to pregnancy problems? Teenage girls seeking an abortion obviously have a problem with pregnancy, and the counseling task is to help her understand and face her own psychological and moral dimensions of that decision (41). The choice for abortion ought not be made causally, but responsibly and probably even reluctantly. We need to recognize that undue emphasis on the mechanics of abortion and statistical morality can prevent us from grasping and dealing with this issue fully.

The psychological and social problem with abortion, as with any other conflict of life-against-life, is chiefly the question of how to balance rights – in this case, the rights of the unborn against the rights of a woman. That conflict has long been recognized in western culture and western medicine, but in ways which do not now appear to be compelling in the present situation. Indeed, the tendency in our recent past has been to deny that there is any genuine conflict – by describing abortion as a "procedure" (which suggests that it is only a technical matter) or as "therapeutic" (which suggests that the fetus is a disease and locates benefit in a woman without acknowledging that the minimal good cure is a very dead fetus) or as "a woman's right to control her body" (which nullifies in principle all talk about the sanctity of life of the unborn). To point out these ways in which rhetoric shields behavior is only to remind us that, in the present situation, we seem to want somehow to deny what happens in every abortion – and that is that a fetus is killed when a valuing choice is acted on in the face of apparently irreconcilable conflict.

Acknowledging that primary fact does not (to our mind) overcome all the reasons for this action which are put forward by advocates of abortion on request. On the other hand, acknowledging that fact should invest all the other reasons with a gravity and solemnity that they otherwise appear to want. We need not brutalize our already eroded moral sensibilities in order to act responsibly and honestly in the face of such conflict. Sometimes, within the limits of finite choice and apparently irreconcilable conflict between lives, we do not doubt that abortion is preferable to the conditions which would otherwise prevail in the absence of abortion (42). And to understand that this decision is a matter of preference, with all the tragedy and pain and relief and benefit that attends it, may assist us to make hard choices like this without sacrificing the rudimentary consciousness of our essential humanity.

ABORTION COUNSELING

Generally, those girls are more ambivalent about abortion who are frightened, who lack an adequate self-concept, who must deal with unhelpful parents, and who are not involved in a mature love relationship — those girls will need extensive counseling after, as well as before, abortion. Preabortion counseling has ordinarily been perfunctory or desultory; and postabortion counseling has been virtually nonexistent. Hopefully more extensive counseling than has typically been offered will prevent another unwanted pregnancy, with all the anguish and torment which usually accompanies it. If successful, counseling will help the young girl to redirect her life into more mature and responsible relationships. The following case report illustrates.

N. was a very neurotic girl who was impregnated by an older divorced man. She was referred for abortion evaluation during the fourteenth week of her pregnancy. She had refused to tell her parents until she was informed that she needed the consent of at least one of them for an abortion. During the initial interview she indicated her ambivalence about the abortion. "It must be a crime to start a pregnancy you don't want to go through," she said. "I don't want this baby, but every time I think about it I feel sorry for myself." She had recurrent "blue" periods, crying spells, insomnia, and anorexia (her weight loss was twelve pounds in two months). Of her mother, she said somewhat contemptuously, "Mother will make the best of it because she likes to think she's invincible." She had told her mother, "I'm sorry to burden you with this, but there was nothing else I could do."

The mother described N. as a quiet child, always eager to please, who had lived in the shadow of an older sister who was beautiful, popular, and extremely talented. The mother was the forceful, dominant person in the family. The father was quiet, sympathetic, and concerned. Interestingly, he never displayed any anger toward the man who was party to the unhappy episode.

N. suffered from an extremely poor self-concept. She considered the pregnancy to be additional evidence of her failure as a person — she had disappointed her parents, her companion had terminated the affair and then deserted her in her crisis. Following the abortion, she urgently needed counseling regarding her tendency to get involved with such people. She refused counseling but accepted contraceptives.

Within six months she was readmitted after a suicidal attempt which was prompted by an unhappy love affair. On the ward she was initially withdrawn. She constantly found fault with all female staff members, but was seductive with the young male staff. She tried to control her treatment, refusing to go to group therapy or physical therapy. She became angry with her parents and demanded that the phone be taken out of her room so they could not call her directly. She refused to see her friends. This manipulation so isolated her that she had numerous "panic attacks" which required a staff member to sit with her and literally hold her hand. It became increasingly clear that her disastrous love life was, at least in part, due to her own need to dominate people. She withdrew from personal situations where there was conflict and which made her feel, in turn, not totally in charge. As a result, she selected weak young men whom she could control but who were unable to meet her genuine needs for love and support. A long course of psychotherapy was recommended and, fortunately this time, was accepted.

CONTRACEPTION

Teenagers today are very much influenced by a variety of liberation movements; and since most of these are directed toward the domination of white males, it might be expected that physicians in their practice would experience the impact of these crusades chiefly with women patients. Indeed, some of the newer women's groups are frank to say that they view the traditional fatherly role of the doctor as a mysogynist attitude which functions to deny women freedom as individuals. So given the natural history of human reproduction, together with the availability of male contraceptives over-the-counter, it is not surprising that physicians are sometimes confronted by girls who stride boldly into their consultation rooms and demand contraceptive information and devices.

THE ROLE OF THE PHYSICIAN

Some physician's, faced with this situation, simply send the patient away; others, if they see only the aggression in the girl's manner, deliver a stern lecture which is usually garnished with dire warnings and forebodings of the awful future that lies ahead for a fallen woman. If the physician feels particularly sadistic that day, he can – without permission of the patient, or adequate professional reflection – pick up the telephone and call the girl's parents. This response, which can be admittedly provoked by the girl's arrogance, is nevertheless self-serving behavior which is not in keeping with the Hippocratic admonition to heal and comfort.

At the other end of the spectrum, the "liberated" physician, who strongly believes in placing autonomous decision-making in the hands of the young, may reply "of course" to such a demand, conduct a physical examination, write the appropriate prescription for his preferred contraceptive, and thereafter firmly eschew any further responsibility for the patient's psychologic well-being. With such an attitude as this, the doctor usually fails to probe deeply into the reasons – other than the superficial request – for the girl's presence in his office.

The stance of both sorts of physicians is mistaken, not so much for what they did but for what they failed to do. There are surely patients who need a lecture, just as there are patients who need contraceptives prescribed. But the error of these doctors was in failing to deal with the patient as an individual person – failing to take the time to assess her psychological health, to inquire in a tactful manner about her familiarity with sexual matters, to ask about her relationships with boys, her future intentions, her fears of pregnancy, her relationships with parents, and other cognate matters.

For the most part, this kind of professional response suggests a departure from the physician's traditionally dominant role to a more understanding acceptance of the patient's display of arrogance and superiority. This different role is uncomfortable — for who wants to hear demands or receive an ultimatum? — and it is very easy to reject such patients. Indeed, these patients often have intense and unrealistic fears of their own dependency yearnings which they seek to relieve by controlling or dominating the physician. If the doctor can deal with this in an unembarrassed and friendly manner, he will be well on his way to developing a trusting relationship with the girl. Moreover, armed with this information, he is much better equipped to deal with the decisions that have to be made. Physicians who accept the principle of premarital virginity, for example, must have tolerance for other points of view if they are to address themselves to the real sexual problem of some young girls. These patients hope to avoid pregnancy and that seems to them a responsible attitude.

The conception control instrument of choice is usually "the pill," although many authorities have advised caution in its use with adolescents. Some experts state that only the minipill and the sequential pill should be used in this age group, and that the prescription should be only for short periods of time so that the girl can be evaluated for side effects. We know that reactions usually depend on the type of pill prescribed, and that those with excess estrogen cause such symptoms as gastrointestinal disorders, nausea, increased weight as a result of edema, and breast tension. Excess gestagen, on the other hand, may lead to increased appetite, anabolic weight increase, tiredness, depression, and decreased libido. In addition, it has been demonstrated that a statistically significant association exists between use of oral contraceptives and such serious reactions as thrombophlebitis, pulmonary embolism, and cerebral thrombosis (43). With such an imposing list of side effects the importance of a frank, trusting relationship with the girl cannot be overstated.

Other methods of contraception and birth control include intrauterine devices, mechanical devices, spermicides, and biological methods; and all should be carefully considered when the pill is considered unsafe. During the last decade, in particular, there has been a progressive increase in the development and use of intrauterine devices (IUD). While scientists are still trying to determine exactly how these devices work, the fact that a foreign body in the uterus prevents nidation has been known for many generations; and, in fact, it has long been a favorite abortifacient method of prostitutes. Unfortunately, quacks frequently inserted the devices without taking adequate sterility precautions. Thus the incidence of infection and perforation of the uterus was very high and the use of IUD's fell into disrepute by conservative physicians. Today, with modern plastic devices (the well-known Lippes loop) and aseptic insertion by an expert, the incidence of troublesome side effects is quite low. The major reasons for discontinuance of the loop are: (1) bleeding and/or pain, and (2) expulsion (a small percentage of women, seemingly, cannot retain the loop and expel it back out into the vagina). Some physicians are concerned that such devices might cause infection or cancer, but Lippes loop studies fail to show increases in either infection or cancer rates among women using the loop for many years. The loops are widely used in underdeveloped countries, such as India and Korea, because they are very economical when compared to the "pill" and almost as effective.

Mechanical devices, such as the diaphragm, serve as obstructive barriers to the passage of sperm into the uterus. The condom is simply a flexible rubber sheath placed over the penis that collects the semen. Improper fitting of diaphragms and tears in condoms are the hazards that make them relatively less effective than the "pill" or IUD's.

Chemical spermicides are usually creams inserted with an applicator stick just prior to intercourse. The cream is deposited near the cervix where, hopefully, it kills any sperm that seek passage. Some physicians advise simultaneous use of diaphragms with chemical spermicides. But both mechanical and chemical methods are unpopular because they are annoying restraints to spontaneity. Couples have to interrupt their lovemaking in order for the woman to insert the diaphragm and/or cream, or for the man to roll on the condom.

The rhythm method is, of course, the least reliable of the conception control methods. Ovulation usually occurs on the fourteenth day prior to the next period. The morning temperature is ordinarily elevated on that day and, for this reason, women who are trying to get pregnant are frequently advised by their physician to chart carefully their morning temperature and then have intercourse as soon thereafter as possible. The same facts can be used conversely to avoid pregnancy. If a woman abstains from intercourse from the nineteenth through the ninth day prior to her next period, she should be infertile. In women who are very regular, the method is sound. For unexplained reasons, ovulation can vary (some women even ovulate while they are menstruating); and therefore the rhythm method frequently fails. There is some truth to the old saw: "Couples who practice rhythm are called parents." Nevertheless, this is a very important method, if only because it is the sole form of conception control officially sanctioned by the Roman Catholic Church for its more than 400 million members.

Many teenagers have dangerous misconceptions about rhythm. It is not uncommon for them to think that conception occurs only on the day of ovulation. Most teenagers will have little knowledge of other contraceptive techniques; yet, in selected circumstances, one or another of these techniques may be preferable. There are still different methods of contraception currently under investigation – some at the stage of clinical testing – which may become available in the future. These experimental methods include suppression of ovulation for varying periods by injections of estrogen-progesterones at monthly or perhaps longer intervals. In Melbourne, Australia, some promiscuous girls who are wards of the court are now being given such long-acting contraceptive injections with the consent of the girl, or of her parents when she is under sixteen. The contraceptive in this case is medroxy-progesterone acetate. Its ultimate usefulness awaits further study.

STERILIZATION

When nonsurgical methods for conception control fail or entail uncommonly high risks, some persons turn to sterilization as a second line of defense against unwanted pregnancy. In the normal course of events, teenagers do not seek sterilization; and when they do, this alternative is ordinarily sought with some reluctance. Studies show that hesitancy to submit to surgical sterilization is rooted in a constellation of factors: these procedures are almost always irreversible, they do not enjoy widespread social acceptance as the method of choice, certain legal restrictions apply, and there is more psychological and philosophical ambivalence toward surgical than nonsurgical means for conception control.

Nevertheless we do occasionally see young people who seriously consider a sterilizing procedure. One of these was a sexually active male college student who, not uncharacteristically of his peer group, was passionately committed to a cause — in this case, the goal of zero population growth. The physician rightly suspected that this ardent young man wanted to discharge his social obligation to the population crisis with a single, noble deed; and, moreover, that he needed only to be provided with a reputable and reliable means for doing so. In their conversation, the doctor (wisely, we think) advised this student to postpone such a decision and cited, among other reasons, a possible lack of fairness to his mate should the boy eventually decide to marry.

More frequently, requests for teenage sterilization come from retarded persons, their parents, or legal guardians. R. was born with a hydrocephalic condition which was successfully treated but left residual brain damage. His parents were well-to-do, prominent people in their community who understood and acknowledged their son's retardation. R. attended public schools and, as it often happens with these youngsters, was graduated for social rather than academic promotion. He was then employed in the family business, and the parents hired someone to supervise his activities. They tried to shield him from assuming any independent responsibility, and only very reluctantly consented to allow him to drive a car. R. first took an active interest in girls at about age fifteen and thereafter he dated sporadically. The parents were aware that he masturbated frequently; and on one occasion he made inappropriate sexual advances to a female relative which alarmed them. They then became very concerned that the boy would father an illegitimate child and brought him to their family doctor with the request that he be sterilized. They reached this decision without consulting R.

The consulting psychologist discovered that R. was indeed limited (IQ=74). He noted, moreover, that R. had somewhat exaggerated opinions of his own capabilities, while at the same time he seemed insecure in his dealings with people. The psychologist also thought the family to be overprotective, and suggested that the family talk over their decision with R. prior to proceeding.

Several years later R. brought himself to the mental health clinic. He had many concerns he wished to talk about: he felt that people, specifically girls, did not like him; he thought that his parents had a low opinion of him, and he particularly wanted to prove himself to his father but was unsure of how to proceed; and he hoped someday to marry and have children as his father did before him. It remains yet to be seen whether R. can accomplish his goals, but overprotection from both parents and society have been (and can continue to be) impediments to their achievement.

Many people have, of course, distorted concepts of mental retardation, and the victims of this disability are therefore frequently accorded subhuman status. The fact is, however, that many retarded people are perfectly capable of emotional development to adulthood. They are able to form mature relationships and to care adequately for children. Accordingly we believe that an opportunity to participate in the decisions that affect their lives, contingent on their ability to understand, should be a vital part of any treatment plan for them.

An even more frequent situation is compulsory sterilization of handicapped teenagers. More than half of our states now have laws which provide for eugenic sterilization, both voluntary and involuntary, of certain persons whether adult or minor. All of these statutes further designate the retarded as subject to sterilization; and in many instances, insanity and epilepsy are also included (although in several states, epilepsy has recently been removed from the list of prescribed subjects).

Every state which practices compulsory vaccination already sustains the principle that some private and personal right must be subordinated to the public and general welfare. And every state institution for mental defectives which segregates male and female inmates already practices *de facto* sterilization. But the Nazi atrocities, together with recent abuses in our own country, should be adequate reminder that the power of the state to sterilize compulsorily ought to be restricted in the most careful ways.

SURGICAL TECHNIQUES

Vasectomy is the surgical technique for sterilizing men and can be done under local anesthetic in a urologist's office. In this procedure, which normally takes about five minutes, the tube (vas deferens) which carries seminal fluid containing the sperm from the testis to the ejaculatory duct is tied off or cut. Vasectomy prevents discharge of the vital secretion of the testes, but there is no ill effect on the production of other chemical substances or the function of other glands and organs. This operation has been advocated as an ideal method of conception control because it is simple, cheap and effective; and surveys have shown that as many as two percent of the married male population in the United States undergo vasectomy. The complications of the procedure are rare, although men report mild pain and, occasionally, discomfort in the testes.

Sterilizing surgery for women is somewhat more complex and usually involves an abdominal operation. In skilled hands it is a safe and effective operation. The ordinary method is salpingectomy and accomplished by ligation (either cutting or tying) of the Fallopian tubes, which carry ova from the ovaries to the uterus. As in the case of vasectomy, salpingectomy simply prevents passage between two essential points in the reproductive system. More serious, and less commonly done for sterilization alone, is excision of the uterus itself or hysterectomy. A new and promising method that will probably become the standard procedure in the future is laparoscopic tubal ligation. In this procedure, the physician inserts a fiberoptic viewing instrument through a small umbilical incision which, in turn, allows visualization of the tubes in the pelvic cavity. Through another small incision an instrument is inserted and, guided by the laparoscope, cauterizes and divides the tubes. This method is safe and economical, and requires only one day of hospitalization.

PSYCHOLOGICAL REACTIONS TO STERILIZING SURGERY

It is important to understand that neither the testes in

vasectomy, nor the ovaries in tubal ligation, are disturbed; and that therefore neither of these operations involve or can be called castration. Nor do either of these procedures interfere with the physiological aspects of sexual intercourse itself. There may be certain psychological affects, but most of these can be credited to unfortunate cultural stereotypes which equate sterilization with castration. Some men are (mistakenly) apprehensive about possible loss of their masculinity; and many women, particularly after hysterectomy, tend to have feelings of inferiority and sometimes frank depression because they (falsely) equate fecundity with womanhood. The facts are that, owing to removal of the fear of pregnancy, frequency of intercourse and increase in libido often occur after a sterilizing procedure. These operations, when voluntarily elected, have the same effect as efficient contraceptives.

EPILOGUE

ALTHOUGH we have given primary attention to the sexual difficulties of promiscuous teenagers in this study, we have also undertaken throughout to indicate that the meaning and purpose of sexual behavior is not always obvious and that we are sometimes mistaken if we suppose that certain objective actions invariably correlate with certain subjective meanings. To put it another way: we are on very dangerous ground if we allow personal aversion to or contempt for the promiscuous teenager's behavior to prejudice, and therefore compromise, our resources for therapy.

So it is partly in order to treat this patient as an individual person, as well as to gain the information which is requisite to understanding what is problematic in a given case, that we have argued (as though it needed arguing!) the necessity for a detailed inquiry into the patient's life history before consideration of a treatment regimen. To know how the patient views himself in relation to the significant others in his life, and to ascertain what important psycholgical needs the patient satisfies by sexual behavior, are illustrations of the kind of information we must have if we are to understand whether the teenager's sexual life is promiscuous or healthy, whether it signals a disturbed person engaged in destructive covenants or a well-adjusted person participating in relationships which facilitate growth. In cases of teenage promiscuity we are dealing with deeply troubled young-sters who may (and probably do) need psychiatric care and treatment.

INSTITUTES

A psychiatric hospital offers a therapeutic milieu which facilitates the patient's recovery by providing a staff which is

90

trained to view each interaction with patients as potentially helpful in the recovery process. Somewhat paradoxically, the most important persons in the recovery process are often the lowest paid, least educated, and humblest ranking staff — the aides and attendants who supervise the daily life of hospitalized teenagers, arbitrate disputes, supervise recreation, help with homework, maintain discipline, and listen to grievances.

Because education is such an integral part of each teenager's life good residential treatment centers provide trained teachers and space for a school. Social workers perform the principal communication function with families, assist in family therapy, and work with community agencies to provide aftercare. Nurses, in addition to regular nursing duties, supervise aides and attendants, hold ward community meetings, and assist in group therapy. Psychologists administer and interpret tests which measure cognitive faculties, self-concepts, and personality features. Many additional persons are trained to function as individual and group psychotherapists. Psychiatrists are almost always the admitting officers and responsible for the overall evaluation, care, and eventual disposition of the patient. They must devise a workable treatment plan, the execution of which may be delegated to other staff members whom they supervise. In addition, they may do individual psychotherapy, group therapy, and family therapy. Staff conferences are necessary to share observations of the patients, detail treatment progress, and reformulate treatment plans.

In the course of one week a hospitalized teenager may attend school four hours per day, Monday through Friday, attend ward meetings twice weekly, attend group therapy once weekly, visit an individual therapist twice weekly, participate in family conferences, attend supervised recreation daily, go to dances several times weekly, and make a home visit.

We have described in some detail the hospital environment for a number of reasons. First, promiscuous teenagers are often hospitalized in order to control their sexual "acting out." Second, good hospitals require large numbers of well-trained staff who are closely supervised, and such care is therefore expensive. Third, treatment which is designed around the concept of increasing self-awareness, promoting self-esteem, and facilitating the onset of personal maturity takes time, often many months, to produce more responsible behavior. Fourth, custodial hospitals may exert a deleterious affect on troubled teenagers through the phenomena of institutionalism (44) which may engender lowered human dignity, apathy, boredom, loss of spontaneity, and further regression to even more primitive modes of behavior.

The decision to hospitalize is therefore a very serious one which needs to take into account the availability of suitable resources to help the patient, the patient's capacity to profit from treatment, and the family's willingness to participate in a comprehensive treatment program.

PARENTS

In our experience we have found that it is important to talk with parents separately, at least for the first interview or two. This arrangement allows the parents, independently of each other and the teenage patient, to ventilate their pent-up rage and frustration

Figure 14. Drawing by teenage boy.

without further injury to the teenager's self-esteem; and we have found that subsequent family discussions tend to be more productive as a result of this opportunity to express true, but heretofore unexpressed feelings. Many times, of course, the parents are so angry that they are not yet ready for professional advice. Thus they may try occasionally to gain the physician's complicity in punishment for the teenager even before the case evaluation can be completed.

Many parents can benefit from participation in a "parent's group," where they can talk out their problem with empathetic listeners and be reassured and supported by awareness that other people like themselves have similarly troubled teenagers. The usual purpose of these groups is for parents to teach each other how to deal constructively with teenage problems. Some parents of troubled teenagers, as we have shown, also have rather severe marital disturbances which, in these groups, are called to consciousness in ways the couple had not previously acknowledged. In these cases, marital counseling for parents may need to complement the treatment regimen for the teenager.

PSYCHOTHERAPY

The development of a successful psychotherapeutic relationship with a skilled therapist will ordinarily produce gratifying remission of the teenager's sexual difficulties. Such a relationship is not always easy to achieve with teenagers, however, because their interpersonal difficulties with trust and authority make them guarded (if not suspicious) in relationships with adults. Indeed, teenagers with severely damaged self-concepts tend to project blame for all their troubles onto others; and physicians are especially susceptible to a rebellious teenager's attempt to subvert the therapeutic alliance into a weapon for bludgeoning parents. So long as other persons can be seen as the source and sustenance of "the problem," the teenager can employ this projective mechanism to avoid looking into himself for remedy.

GROUP THERAPY

Like parents' groups, peer group relationships for teenagers can provide a valuable resource for promoting desired change. With younger teenagers it is preferable to segregate sexes because the girls tend to dominate discussions. Older teenagers, however, ordinarily profit from a balanced heterosexual group.

Discussion in both younger and older groups tend to focus on relations with parents; and some therapists use role-playing techniques in order to dramatize and teach teenagers to appreciate the difficulties and complexities of parenthood.

We have endeavored throughout this book to avoid the use of formal psychiatric diagnoses to categorize troubled teenagers. Certainly it is true that many sexually active teenagers have disturbances in thinking, feeling, and behaving which fall into psychiatric diagnostic categories. Our purpose, however, was not taxonomy. Rather, we have sought throughout to explore the sexual life of promiscuous teenagers in terms of the responsible decision making to which the teenager, the physician, and others who deal with young people are party. We have discussed psychological and medical processes only when these discussions clarified the nature of the decisions to be made, and the choices which were available. In this manner we have wanted to engender more generally responsible decision making about sexual matters because we believe that persons endeavor to humanize their relationships, that they wish to carry within themselves the picture of an estimable human being.

BIBLIOGRAPHY

1. Zelnik, M. and Kantner, J.F.: Sexuality, contraception, and pregnancy among young unwed females in the United States. In Westoff, G.F. and Parke, R. (Eds): Demographic and Social Aspects of Population Growth. Washington, U.S. Government Printing Office, 1972.
2. – – –: The probability of premarital intercourse. Soc Sci Res, 1:335-339, 1972.
3. Kinsey, A. C., Pomeroy, W.B. and Martin, C.E.: Sexual Behavior in the Human Male. Philadelphia, Saunders, 1948.
4. Kinsey, A.C.: Sexual Behavior in the Human Female. By the staff of the Institute for Sexual Research. Philadelphia, Saunders, 1953.
5. Masters, W.H. and Johnson, V.E.: Human Sexual Response. Boston, Little, Brown, 1966.
6. – – –: Human Sexual Inadequacy. Boston, Little, Brown, 1970.
7. Williams, T.: The yellow bird. In One Arm and Other Stories. New York, New Directions, 1954.
8. Money, J. and Ehrhardt, A.A.: Psychosexual Differentiation. Baltimore, Johns Hopkins Press, 1972.
9. Federman, D.D.: Abnormal Sexual Development. A Genetic and Endocrine Approach to Differential Diagnosis. Philadelphia, Saunders, 1967.
10. Levin, M.: Psychiatric notes. Curr Med Dialog, September, 1968.
11. Graham, E.: Now the boy inkblots look like girl blots and that says a lot. Wall Street Journal, August 20, 1971.
12. Erikson, E.H.: Identity, Youth and Crisis. New York, Norton, 1968.
13. Dai, B.: A socio-psychiatric approach to personality organization. Am Soc Rev, 17:1, 1952.
14. Knapp, J.J.: Alternative marriage styles: An exploratory study of co-marital sex and flexible role structures. Presented at Meeting of Southern Sociological Society, Atlanta, 1973.
15. Rimmer, R.K.: The Harrad Experiment. New York, Bantam Books, 1968.
16. O'Neill, N. and O'Neill, G.C.: Open Marriage: A New LIfe Style for Couples. New York, Evans, 1972.
17. Morris, D.: The Human Zoo. New York, McGraw Hill, 1969.
18. 1970 Census of the Population: Detailed Characteristics U.S. Summary issued 1973, pp. 1, 640-641.
19. Anderson, W.S. and Latts, S.M.: High school marriages and school policies in Minnesota. J Marriage, 27:266-270, 1965.

96   *The Promiscuous Teenager*

20. Lowrie, S.H.: Early marriage: Premarital pregnancy and associated factors. J Marriage, 27:48-56, 1965.
21. LaBarre, M. and LaBarre, W.: The triple crisis: Adolescence, early marriage and parenthood, part I – Motherhood. In The Double Jeopardy: The Triple Crisis. New York, National Council on Illegitimacy, 1969, pp. 9-33.
22. LaBarre, M.: Services for school age expectant married couples. Presented at the Annual Meeting of The American Orthopsychiatric Association, Detroit, 1972.
23. Powell, I.R.: Teenage Marital Units: A Descriptive Study. Dissertation, University of North Carolina at Greensboro, 1973.
24. LaBarre, M.: Pregnancy experiences among married adolescents. Am J Orthopsychiat, 38:47-55, 1968.
25. Pannor, R., Massarik, F. and Evans, B.: The Unmarried Father. New York, Springer, 1970.
26. Beiber, I., et al.: Homosexuality: A Psychoanalytic Study by Irving Beiber and Others. New York, Basic Books, 1962.
27. Marmour, J.: Sexual Inversion: The Multiple Roots of Homosexuality. New York, Basic Books, 1965, pp. 1-26.
28. Freud, S.: Letter to an American mother. Am J Psychiat, 107:786-787, 1951.
29. Bergler, E.: Homosexuality, Disease or Way of Life? New York, Hill and Wang, 1956.
30. Teal, D.: The Gay Militants. New York. Stein and Day, 1971.
31. Berg, C. and Allen, C.: The Wolfenden Report. New York, Citadel Press, 1958.
32. Johnson, M. and Szurek, A.R.: The genesis of antisocial acting out in children and adults. Psychoanal Q, 21:323-343, 1952.
33. Schroeter, A.L. and Lucas, J.B.: Gonorrhea – Diagnosis and treatment. Obstet Gynecol, 39:274-285, 1972.
34. Rudolph, A.H.: Control of gonorrhea. JAMA, 220:1587-1589, 1972.
35. Tietze, C. Pakter, Jean, and Berger, G.: Mortality with legal abortion in New York City, 1970-1972. JAMA, 225:507-509, 1973.
36. The Right to Abortion: A Psychiatric View, GAP Publication, New York, 1972.
37. Pfeiffer, E.: Psychiatric indications of psychiatric justification of therapeutic abortion? Arch Gen Psychiat, 23:402-407, 1970.
38. Chase, G.: Report from the Health Services Administration of the City of New York. Presented to the National Association for Repeal of Abortion Laws, Detroit, 1972.
39. Rowe versus Wade: citation 410US113, 1973.
40. Doe versus Bolton: citation 410US179, 1973.
41. Perez-Reyes, M.G., and Falk, R.: Follow-up after therapeutic abortion in early adolescence. Psychiat Digest, 34:12, 1973.
42. Smith, H.: Ethics and the New Medicine. Nashville, Abingdon Press, 1970.

43. Heyman, A. et al.: Oral contraception and increased risk of cerebral ischemia or thrombosis. By the Collaborative Group for the Study of Stroke in Young Women. N Engl J Med, 288:871-878, 1973.
44. Goffman, I.: Asylums: Essays on The Social Situation of Mental Patients and Other Inmates. Garden City, Doubleday, 1961.

INDEX

Sexual urges, 23
Sexuality,
 casual, 58
 human, 36, 42
 indiscriminate, 58
 marital, 40
 open, 37
 promiscuous, 58
 teenage, vii
 xomatic, 19
Sexy, 39
Sterilization, 85-88
 compulsory, 87
 de facto, 87
 eugenic, 87
 surgical, 85
 teenage, 86
Sterilizing surgery, psychological reactions to, 88, 89
Stimulated, sexually, 41
Stimulation, breast, 23
Strivings, erotic, 26, 52-55
Styles, sexual, 37
Subcultures, homosexual, 50
Subhuman status, 87
Suicidal observation, 27
Suppression of ovulation, 85
Surgery, sterilizing, 88
Surgical sterilization, 85
Surgical techniques, 88
Surrender, sexual, 32
Surrogate, mother, 65
Symptoms
 neurotic, 28
 venereal, 14
Synergamist, 39
Synergamy and open marriage, 38-40
Sexually active, 63
Sexually active teenagers, 73
Sexually segregated school, 25
Sexually stimulated, 41
Situations, social, 24
Smith, H., 96
Society, 24
 gay, 53
Social and political crises, 4
Social concourse, 24
Social conscience, 28
Social prohibitions, 67
Social dimensions, vii
Social situations, 24

Social workers, 91
Sodomy, 49, 56
"Speed," 61
Sperm, 88
Spermicides, 83
 chemical, 84
Standards, premarital sex, 58
Statistical normality, 48
Stereotypes, cultural, 89
Sterility precautions, 84
Syphilis, 70
 congenital, 70
Syphilitic mother, 70
Szurek, A. R., 96

T

Teal, O., 96
Techniques, role-playing, 94
Teenage marriage, 43-45
Teenage patient, 92
Teenage pregnancy, 73
Teenage sterilization, 86
Teenagers
 sexually active, 73
 submissive, 17
 unwed pregnant, 71
Tender nipples, 75
Tension, sexual, 24, 67
Term delivery, 75
Testes, 88
Testing, psychological, 64-66
Tetracyclines, 70
Therapeutic,
 alliance, 93
 milieu, 90
Therapists, 94
Therapy, 55, 56
 family, 91
 games method, 35
 group, 14, 81, 91, 93, 94
 physical, 81
Theories, analytic, 11
Thorough-going behaviorism, 20
Thrombophlebitis, 83
Thrombosis cerebral, 83
Tietze, C. Pakter, 95
Tietze, J., 96
Tiredness, 83
Topless dresses, 7
Training school, 13